LifeLight

"In Him was life, and that life was the light of men." John 1:4

Genesis, Part 1

—

GENESIS 1:1–25:11

LEADERS GUIDE

SAINT LOUIS

Jane L. Fryar, editor

Revised from material prepared by Dean O. Wenthe and Timothy Huber

This publication is available in braille and in large print for the visually impaired. Write to the Library for the Blind, 1333 S. Kirkwood Road, St. Louis, MO 63122-7295; or call 1-800-433-3954.

Cover Illustration: Eric Westbrook

Contents

Introduction

Welcome to LifeLight

A special pleasure is in store for you. You will be instrumental in leading your brothers and sisters in Christ closer to Him who is our life and light (John 1:4). You will have the pleasure of seeing fellow Christians discover new insights and rediscover old ones as they open the Scriptures and dig deep into them, perhaps deeper than they have ever dug before. More than that, you will have the pleasure of sharing in this wonderful study.

LifeLight—An In-depth Study

LifeLight is a series of in-depth Bible studies. The goal of LifeLight is that through a regular program of in-depth personal and group study of Scripture, more and more Christian adults may grow in their personal faith in Jesus Christ, enjoy fellowship with the members of His body, and reach out in love to others in witness and service.

In-depth means that this Bible study includes the following four components: individual daily home study; discussion in a small group; a lecture presentation on the Scripture portion under study; and an enhancement of the week's material (through reading the enrichment magazine).

LifeLight Participants

LifeLight participants are adults who desire a deeper study of the Scriptures than is available in the typical Sunday morning adult Bible class. (Mid-to-older teens might also be LifeLight participants.) While LifeLight does not assume an existing knowledge of the Bible or special experience or skills in Bible study, it does assume a level of commitment that will bring participants to each of the nine weekly assemblies having read the assigned readings and attempted to answer the study questions. Daily reading and study will require from 15 to 30 minutes for the five days preceding the LifeLight assembly. The day following the assembly will be spent reviewing the previous week's study by going over the completed study leaflet and the enrichment magazine.

LifeLight Leadership

While the in-depth process used by LifeLight begins with individual study and cannot achieve its aims without this individual effort, it cannot be completed by individual study alone. Therefore, trained leaders are necessary. You fill one or perhaps more of the important roles described below.

The Director

This person oversees the LifeLight program in a local center (which may be a congregation or a center operated by several neighboring congregations). The director

- serves as the parish LifeLight overall coordinator and leader;
- coordinates the scheduling of the LifeLight program;
- orders materials;
- convenes LifeLight leadership team meetings;
- develops publicity materials;
- recruits participants;
- maintains records and budgeting;
- assigns, with the leadership team, participants to small discussion groups;
- makes arrangements for facilities;
- communicates outreach opportunities to small-group leaders and to congregational boards;
- follows up on participants who leave the program.

The Assistant Director *(optional)*

This person may assist the director. Duties listed for the director may be assigned to the assistant director as mutually agreeable.

The Lecture Leader

This person prepares and delivers the lecture at the weekly assembly. **(Lesson material for the lecture leader begins on p. 9.)** The lecture leader

- prepares and presents the Bible study lecture to the large group;

- prepares worship activities (devotional thought, hymn, prayer), using resources in the study leaflet and leaders guide and possibly other outside sources;

- helps the small-group discussion leaders to grow in understanding the content of the lessons;

- encourages prayer at weekly leadership team and discussion leaders meetings.

The Small-Group Coordinator *(optional; the director may fill this role)*

This person supervises and coordinates the work of the small-group discussion leaders. The small-group coordinator

- recruits with the leadership team the small-group discussion leaders;

- trains or arranges for training of the discussion leaders;

- assists the director and discussion leaders in follow-up and outreach;

- encourages the discussion leaders to contact absent group members;

- participates in the weekly leadership team and discussion leaders equipping meetings;

- provides ongoing training and support as needed.

The Small-Group Discussion Leaders

These people guide and facilitate discussion of LifeLight participants in the small groups. **(Lesson material for the small-group leaders begins on p. 63.)** There should be one discussion leader for every group of no more than 12 participants. The small-group discussion leaders are, perhaps, those individuals who are most important to the success of the program. They should, therefore, be chosen with special care and be equipped with skills needed to guide discussion and to foster a caring fellowship within the group. These discussion leaders

- prepare each week for the small-group discussion by using the study leaflet and small-group leaders guide section for that session **(see p. 63)**;

- read the enrichment magazine as a study supplement;

- guide and facilitate discussion in their small group;

- encourage and assist the discussion group in prayer;

- foster fellowship and mutual care within the discussion group;

- attend weekly discussion leaders training meetings.

Leadership Training

LifeLight leaders will meet weekly to review the previous week's work and plan the coming week. At this session, leaders can address concerns and prepare for the coming session. LifeLight is a 1½-hour program with no possibility for it to be taught in the one hour typically available on Sunday mornings. Some congregations, however, may want to use the Sunday morning Bible study hour for LifeLight preparation and leadership training. In such a meeting, the lecture leader and/or small-group coordinator may lead the discussion leaders through the coming week's lesson, reserving 5 or 10 minutes for problem solving or other group concerns.

While it requires intense effort, LifeLight has proven to bring great benefit to LifeLight participants. The effort put into this program, both by leaders and by participants, will be rewarding and profitable.

The LifeLight Weekly Schedule

Here is how LifeLight will work week by week:

1. Before session 1, each participant will receive the study leaflet for session 1 and the enrichment magazine for the course. The study leaflet contains worship resources (for use both in individual daily study and at the opening of the following week's assembly) and readings and study questions for five days. Challenge questions will lead those participants who have the time and desire a greater challenge into even deeper levels of study.

2. After the five days of individual study at home, participants will gather for a weekly assembly of all LifeLight participants. The assembly will begin with a brief period of worship (5 minutes). Participants will then join their assigned small discussion groups (of 12 or fewer, who will remain the same throughout the course), where they will go over the week's study questions together (55 minutes). Assembling together once again, participants will listen to a lecture presentation on the readings they have studied in the previous week and discussed in their small groups (20 minutes). After the lecture presentation, the director or another leader will distribute the study leaflet for the following week. Closing announcements and other necessary business may take another five minutes before dismissal.

In some places some small groups will not join the weekly assembly because of scheduling or other reasons. Such groups may meet at another time and place (perhaps in the home of one of the small group's members). They will follow the same schedule, but they may use the music CD to join in singing the opening hymn and a cassette tape to listen to the week's lecture presentation. The discussion leader will obtain the tape and leaflets from the director. A cassette tape version of the lecture is available for purchase from CPH (see your catalog). Or a congregation may record the lecture given by the lecture leader at the weekly assembly and duplicate it for use by other groups meeting later in the week.

3. On the day following the assembly, participants will review the preceding week's work by rereading the study leaflet they completed (and that they perhaps supplemented or corrected during the discussion in their small group) and by reading appropriate articles in the enrichment magazine.

Then the LifeLight weekly study process will begin all over again!

Recommended Study Resources for Genesis

Concordia Self-Study Bible, New International Version. St. Louis: Concordia Publishing House, 1986. Interpretive notes on each page form a running commentary on the text. The book includes cross-references, a 35,000-word concordance, full-color maps, charts, and time lines.

Delitzsch, Franz. *A New Commentary on Genesis.* 2 vols. Edinburgh: T. & T. Clark, 1899. A careful handling of theological issues in Genesis, making purposeful use of both Hebrew and Aramaic. A valuable resource.

Leupold, Herbert C. *Exposition of Genesis.* 2 vols. Grand Rapids: Baker Book House, 1942. This commentary is a careful exposition by a conservative scholar.

Luther, Martin. Lectures on Genesis. *Luther's Works.* 8 vols. Edited by Jaroslav Pelikan and Helmut T. Lehmann. St. Louis: Concordia Publishing House, 1958–70. Rather lengthy comments but patient, discerning reading of these volumes is rewarding.

Roehrs, Walter R., and Martin H. Franzmann. *Concordia Self-Study Commentary.* St. Louis: Concordia Publishing House, 1979. This one-volume commentary on the Bible contains 950 pages.

Genesis: The Beginning of Life and Light

Preparing for the Session

Central Focus

Because this is an introductory lesson, the focus is as much on the group as it is on the Book of Genesis. Questions are geared toward introducing Genesis while welcoming LifeLight participants.

Objectives

That the participant, as a child of God and with the Holy Spirit's help, will be led to

1. see a connection between God's purposes for creation and His purposes for our daily life;

2. grasp the primary purpose of all Scripture, including the purpose of Genesis;

3. understand the basic subject matter covered in the Book of Genesis;

4. contribute to a sense of rapport and commitment among the members of the LifeLight group.

Note for small-group leaders: Lesson notes and other materials you will need begin on page 65.

For the Lecture Leader

The first lecture in this series becomes one of the most important messages you will deliver. It sets the tone for the presentations in the weeks ahead and will have the greatest influence on new participants, who may still be apprehensive about their commitment to in-depth Bible study. Prepare well, pray hard, and God's Spirit will be upon you, blessing every word you say.

Here are five steps for you to follow as you prepare to present the lecture effectively each week:

Step 1: Pray for God's blessing and for the guiding presence and help of the Holy Spirit. Know that you have a part in transmitting God's own holy Word. Speak that Word boldly.

Step 2: Read and study God's Word yourself. The Word will strengthen your own faith and life in Christ. The Word will also make you a faithful witness. Study Genesis as a LifeLight participant. Read the daily assignment and answer the study questions. Take part in a discussion group.

Step 3: Prepare your presentations carefully. If possible, make the presentation in your own words, using the printed lecture as a guide that you follow closely. If you do read the printed lecture, practice reading it several times so you are thoroughly familiar with it and can read it fluently in your own presentation style. Know it well enough to maintain eye contact with your audience. You do not need to stick to the printed words slavishly. Say it the way you would say it. Substitute your own illustrations and applications when these fit your situation or audience better.

If your congregation has classes throughout the week, consider making an audiotape (or even a videotape) of your presentation so that these other classes can listen to it after their small-group discussion. You can also purchase a cassette tape from Concordia Publishing House either to serve as an additional help in preparing your own presentation or as a substitute for your presentation, particularly in a home setting.

Step 4: Ask someone in your audience to help you by watching and listening for ways in which you might make your presentation more effective. Pick someone who will be a positive and helpful critic.

Step 5: Pray again. Thank God for giving you an opportunity to pass His Word along to others. Ask Him to bless your effort.

For the Director

As the director you recognize the importance of proper facilities and supplies for the success of LifeLight. Even if your group has participated in LifeLight studies before, take nothing for granted. This is a new study, probably with some new participants. Take time to check and double-check everything and always have "Plan B" in your hip pocket (just in case). Of course, make sure that study leaflets for each subsequent session are available for distribution at the proper time.

Session Plan

Worship

Begin the session with the hymn, devotion, and prayer. The words of the hymn and prayer are printed in the study leaflet. Note that accompaniment for the hymn can be found on the music CD that accompanies this course. If you plan to use it, find it on the disk and cue it up before class.

Devotion

Read Genesis 1:1: "In the beginning God created the heavens and the earth."

Let's pretend. Let's pretend you're an archaeologist. One day, you stumble across the end of a braided cord of spun gold buried in the ground. You begin digging to see what is at the end of it, and the deeper you tunnel, the greater your fascination. Through each successive stratum of earth and artifacts come exciting new revelations covering thousands of years of history.

Dr. Nelson Glueck, a leading Palestinian archaeologist of our time, has said, "It may be stated categorically that no archaeological discovery has ever controverted a Biblical reference. Scores of archaeological findings have been made which confirm in clear outline or in exact detail historical statements in the Bible."[1]

Archaeology has shed light on numerous biblical stories, including a number from Genesis. Even the earliest accounts of Genesis square with archaeological research. The exact location of the Garden of Eden will probably always remain a mystery. Yet archaeology establishes the area of Mesopotamia as the cradle of ancient civilization, just as the Book of Genesis says.

Digging into the Book of Genesis not only unearths our origin but also our destination. Woven through the fabric of time and the pages of Scripture is a golden cord, a lifeline to God, that leads us from the creation of the universe to its Savior. In Genesis, from the great prelude "In the beginning" through the history of Joseph, the darkness of humankind's deeds reads like a historical novel—titillating, discouraging, and ever so accurate. Yet, when we find ourselves at the end of our rope, there is no despair after all. The golden cord we follow throughout Genesis eventually leads to a treasure shining bright—the "LifeLight," Jesus Christ. He is the one for whom we have been digging in Scripture all along. As He says, "These are the Scriptures that testify about Me" (John 5:39).

Ultimately, faith rests not in archaeology, but in the inspired Word of God. It is here that we learn of our sin and our Savior. In the words of the evangelist John, "These are written that you may believe that Jesus is the Christ, the Son of God, and that by believing you may have life in His name" (John 20:31). May God bless our excavations in these weeks ahead, knowing that the promises we unearth in Genesis are promises fulfilled in Christ Jesus!

[1]Josh McDowell, *Evidence That Demands a Verdict* (San Bernardino, CA: Here's Life Publishers, 1979), 65.

Lecture Presentation

This lecture also appears on the CD-ROM that accompanies this course. Also look at the PDFFILES directory on the CD-ROM for visual aids available for the course.

Introduction

Have you heard a good story lately? It is hard not to be captivated by the storyteller who catches our interest with artful imagery and calls our imagination to enter the action. Effortlessly and even unconsciously our interest is focused on the chain of events and on the characters who have been caught up in them. If events take a comic turn, our sides can shake with satisfying laughter. If the tale turns tragic, our hearts can hurt as we identify with the experience. Have you had such a good laugh lately? Or have you felt the pain of tragedies near or far?

1 An Important, Meaningful Story

Whatever your answer, Moses has a story for you. This story can make you laugh with joy way down inside. This story can also touch you with a deep sense of suffering and loss. This is, quite simply, the greatest story ever told. It is hard not be caught up in the drama and high adventure of this story.

A. A Story with a Point

In fact, we can safely say that those who are bored with it have never really heard it. Perhaps their minds were somewhere else. Perhaps they thought they were listening, but they heard only the words and missed the message.

When we miss the point of a story, it can't bring us much understanding or pleasure. Sometimes missing the point causes more drastic consequences—some quite painful.

For example, for centuries scholars and students of antiquity had read Homer's grand epics—the *Iliad* and the *Odyssey*—as great literary masterpieces. But near the end of the 19th century, Heinrich Schliemann got the point that so many others had missed. The renowned classical scholar Cyril E. Robinson tells Schliemann's own story in an entertaining way. **You may choose to tell the following story in your own words rather than read it as a quotation from Robinson's book.**

> Born in 1822, the son of a small-town Lutheran minister, Schliemann was fascinated as a boy by the tales his father told him of the Trojan War. Forced to leave school at the age of fourteen to enter a grocer's shop as an apprentice, he never lost the love of learning. One evening a drunken miller came into the grocery shop and recited a hundred lines of Homer. "From that moment," writes Schliemann, "I never ceased to pray to God that by His grace I might yet have the happiness of learning Greek." His prayer received an almost miraculous answer. Leaving the grocer's shop, he became in rapid succession a messenger-boy, a clerk, a merchant, and finally—a millionaire! He was now ready to fulfill the ambition of his childhood. He devoted his life and wealth to searching for remains of Homer's time. Trusting Homer as his guide, Schliemann unearthed a series of cities and satisfied himself that one of these was the Troy of the *Iliad*.

Cyril E. Robinson, *A History of Greece* (London: Methuen & Co., 1964), 4–5.

Even scholars who were skeptical at first eventually became as convinced as Schliemann. The splendid treasures and priceless artifacts combined with other archaeological evidence to convince the learned of that day and of ours! The checkout boy in the grocery had seen what so many professors had missed! The *Iliad* and *Odyssey* were not just entertaining stories; they also described glorious civilizations that had actually existed. The practical result for Schliemann included the pleasure of possessing priceless gold masks, diadems, daggers, and drinking cups. The fame and fortune that came to Schliemann could not have escaped the notice of the scholars of that day who had missed the point of the stories they studied.

It is possible to hear a story but, by missing the point, to miss out on the real benefits the story offers. The story we are about to study has even greater possibilities of practical benefits for those who pay attention and believe what they hear.

Even so, some have heard this story, paid no attention, refused to believe, and gone on quickly to other pursuits. But some keep coming back to hear the account again and again—convinced this story continually gives them fresh insights and new life.

B. A Story with Unique Features

What is this story? Why should we keep on coming back to it? What makes its characters so compelling? How could it possibly move the human heart from laughter to tears and back again?

Several features of this story are unique. First, this story, with all of its triumphs and tragedies, is true! Its names, people, and places are real! Though it reads like a powerful novel, its plot has not been created for effect or entertainment. In fact, the more time we spend with this story, the more clearly its truths will appear. It has that quality of genuineness that rings true to what we ourselves know about life and interpersonal relationships.

Furthermore, this true story is not just about other people. It will not permit us, if we see its point, merely to sit back and observe the action. As we find ourselves caught up in it, we will discover that it changes us as it confronts us with its truth and claims.

What will especially interest each one of us is the discovery that this true story is not just about some far-off people, but it is our own family history. Just as the remembrances of grandparents fascinate us, this history describes for us those episodes and events that have made us what we are. If one of our ancestors migrated from Europe to the United States or Canada, that event, though it happened long ago, is responsible for the fact that we were born in North America and not in Europe. In the same way, this history will reveal a great deal about us as we are right now—and not just where we live but why we think and act the way we do.

Are you ready to hear this true story? Are you ready to meet your past so you might better understand your present? More than this, are you ready to apply this history in such a way that you will find not buried gold or silver, but the greater treasure of a full and free life?

2 Genesis—Its Author and Its Message

A. Meet Moses the Author

Display visual 1A from the CD-ROM here.

This true story is titled Genesis. Its author is a man named Moses. He lived in another place—ancient Egypt—during a different time—around 1500 B.C.—but he describes the very roots of our family tree. He highlights the key events and describes the crucial characters. He hides nothing. He tells the good; he tells the bad. He faces facts and insists we face them too! By listening carefully we will learn not only about our ancestors, but also about ourselves.

This remarkable history will take us as far back as we can go—to the very beginning. It will introduce us to the very first ancestors in the human race. When we face

the facts of our family tree, the whole world will look different. Our first ancestors shaped more than a part of our future; they changed the face of the earth for all future generations.

B. Hear What Moses Tells Us

God groomed Moses for the task of recounting the full sweep of our family history. Moses grew up in Pharaoh's court (Exodus 2:10) and was trained in its literature and learning (Acts 7:22).

Display visual 1B from the CD-ROM here.

Inspired by the Holy Spirit, Moses later used his educational training. As he begins his first book (he wrote five—Genesis, Exodus, Leviticus, Numbers, and Deuteronomy—the "Pentateuch"), he takes us back to the very beginning, telling us about our first parents (Genesis 1:27–28). In doing so, Moses invites us to consider a startling fact: Our first ancestors, Adam and Eve, were created in the image of God! The human race did not spring from some random cosmic process or from a magical convergence of the stars. Our first parents were formed by the action of a personal God (Genesis 2).

Furthermore, Moses emphasizes over and over the goodness of their world (Genesis 1) and the innocence in which they were created (Genesis 2). We come from good parents, parents created in the image of a good God!

Moses' account of our family history brings us face-to-face with the triune God, a God of love and infinite power who created the whole cosmos as a home for His human creatures.

Display visual 1C from the CD-ROM here.

As we continue to follow our family tree from Adam and Eve to Seth, to Noah, and on down the line, every episode will testify to the fact that the God who created us continues until now to be present with His people. The true tale of our family tree cannot be told without constantly stressing His gracious presence. In a profound sense, the chief character in our history is not a particular grandfather or patriarch but God Himself, who created us and who continues to call us.

Precisely at this point many stop listening. They are

frightened by the thought that God created them and is still present in their personal and family life. They would rather keep the closet closed on such a troublesome family skeleton! But, though such fear falls on all of us, we *must keep listening!* And we must urge others not to flee in fright before this fact.

C. Listen to the Story of a Lifeline

Moses' selection of events and the record of God's actions are not meant to frighten us but to fasten our faith on God's grace. To be sure, Genesis makes no effort to sugarcoat the consequences of sin. Furthermore, sin brings death and destruction. Sin denies our history—our origin in God.

While we meet the fact of sin head-on in events such as the flood, we also meet people like Noah who "found favor in the eyes of the LORD" (Genesis 6:8). There have always been those people in our family tree who by His grace "got the point" of God's presence. The purpose of His promise and presence are to offer favor and mercy to all sinners. To confess our parentage in the God of Adam and Abram is to confess that He is gracious.

The story line of our history does not end in defeat and destruction. Genesis asserts that the fall into sin and all the subsequent failures into which God's human creatures fell are to be turned around through the Seed (NIV "offspring") of the woman. The story line of Genesis turns out to be not a litany of death (Genesis 5), but a lifeline (Genesis 12:3). The genealogies lead us from the light of God in creation (Genesis 1) to the light of God in the life of Jesus Christ (Matthew 1). Just as God broke the primeval darkness with the command "Let there be light" (Genesis 1:3), so He has broken the penetrating darkness of sin with the presence of His Son, Jesus Christ, the Life and the Light of the world (John 1:4–5).

We must view the events of Genesis and the events recorded in the inspired Gospels as the same, one, true story. God's gracious promise in Genesis is that the woman's Seed ("offspring") will reverse the dreadful consequences of the fall into sin (Genesis 3:15; 12:1–3; 15:1–6; 22:15–18; 49:8–12). The fulfillment of that promise, first made in Genesis 3:15, is seen in Jesus Christ. We are invited not simply to acknowledge this history as true in its description of the past and the pres-

ent, but to rely on it in faith and to live so as to reflect the light and reality of Christ's life.

By starting at the beginning, Genesis orients us for a full and free life. We now know from where we have come and, accordingly, we can live with purpose and—above all—with the gracious presence of God in Christ.

The title of our Bible study series—LifeLight—underlines the truth that our life is a story that has its beginning in God. Despite the fall of our first parents into the darkness of sin (Genesis 3), God first promised and then sent the light in the life of Jesus of Nazareth (Genesis 3:15; 12:1–3). The gracious aim of this gift of the woman's Seed was that lives begun in God might also find their end in His goodness and presence. Between that beginning and that end, the light of Christ guides and guards against darkness.

Conclusion

Read the true story of Genesis as though it were your history, for it is! Hear it as the great Good News of deliverance in Christ, for it is that too!

The following eight lessons are written from this perspective. They will lead you to chapter 25 and will be followed by another nine lessons in a second LifeLight course on Genesis.

Above all else, you are invited to hear this ancient story in a fresh way. As you join in this history as your own, in episode after episode, you will see the hand of God. That hand delights in lifting the faith of Abram above his failure. It does not seek to crush and kill the children of Adam and Eve. It seeks to give them new life in Christ!

Concluding Activities

Close with a prayer thanking God for the Holy Scriptures, in which He discloses to us His marvelous plan for our salvation through Jesus. Encourage participants to read the article in the enrichment magazine titled " 'In the beginning God created.' " Then make any necessary announcements and distribute study leaflet 2.

Notes

The Lifeline Grows

Genesis 1–2

Preparing for the Session

Central Focus

This lesson focuses on a God who is both powerful and personal, whose awesome Word brought our entire universe into existence, and whose personal touch shaped clay into a man and formed a rib into a woman. Genesis 1 (the more general account of creation) emphasizes God's power, while Genesis 2 (which expands the details about the creation of man) emphasizes His personal touch.

Objectives

That the participant, as a child of God and with the Holy Spirit's help, will be led to

1. marvel at God's almighty power and wisdom in His plan of creation;

2. understand the position of human beings in God's plan of creation;

3. understand the God-intended unique relationship between male and female;

4. grow in a sense of stewardship by examining the components of the creation account.

Note for small-group leaders: Lesson notes and other materials you will need begin on page 68.

For the Lecture Leader

Read through the lecture several times before presenting it to the large group. The theme that will run throughout this course on Genesis is the truth that God established and maintained a lifeline of hope and promise that eventually led to the Messiah. Emphasize this theme as you come across it in the lectures. You will find that this week's lecture also analyzes the

unique cultural setting in which Moses records the true account of the creation of the world.

Session Plan

Worship

Begin the session with the hymn, devotion, and prayer. The words of the hymn and prayer are printed in the study leaflet. Note that accompaniment for the hymn can be found on the music CD that accompanies this course. If you plan to use it, find it on the disk and cue it up before class.

Devotion

Read Genesis 1:2–3: "Now the earth was formless and empty, darkness was over the surface of the deep, and the Spirit of God was hovering over the waters. And God said, "Let there be light.""

Have you ever committed the irony of "thinking the unthinkable"? The evolutionist Sir Arthur Keith once said, "Evolution is unproved and unprovable. Nevertheless, we believe it because the only alternative is special creation, which is *unthinkable*."[1]

As we open the pages of Scripture God challenges us to "think the unthinkable"—namely, that simply by speaking His Word, God created the universe out of nothing. But why should that be so difficult to believe for people who trust in an almighty God who is able to reassemble our molecules in perfect fashion on resurrection day in order for us to live with Him forever? To paraphrase J. B. Phillips, "Is our God too small?"

Biologist Duane Gish says, "Evolution is a fairy tale for adults" (Kennedy, p. 51). Even theistic evolution, which involves God in the evolutionary process, furnishes no satisfactory answer to the causes of sin and death. As well-known churchman Dennis James Kennedy has stated, "In most fairy tales, someone kisses a frog and in a few seconds, it becomes a prince. That's called a fairy tale. In evolution, something kisses a frog and a few million years later, it becomes a prince. That's called science!" (Kennedy, p. 51).

The Christian faith is not based on fairy tales but on history. It centers on a God who fashioned more than a universe; He also fashioned a plan for our lives that finds meaning only in Jesus Christ. Our Creator is experienced at bringing order out of chaos, and He is used to bringing light out of darkness.

Have you seen the light—the eternal light? That light is Jesus Christ, who was present before the creation began and will be seen eternally after this sinful world is destroyed. As Peter said, "We have the word of the prophets made more certain, and you will do well to pay attention to it, as to a light shining in a dark place, until the day dawns and the morning star rises in your hearts" (2 Peter 1:19).

God said, "Let there be light," and there was. May our journey into Genesis lead us to the light of truth—the ability to "think the unthinkable," to realize that God can not only *create* a world but also *save* a world from the darkness of sin.

[1]Dennis James Kennedy, *Why I Believe* (Waco, Texas: Word, 1980), 51.

··

Lecture Presentation

This lecture also appears on the CD-ROM that accompanies this course. Also look at the PDFFILES directory on the CD-ROM for visual aids available for the course.

Introduction

"Where did the world come from?" "When did life begin?" "How do I fit into the structure of the universe?"

Few human beings have escaped the tug of these questions. **Instead of the following, you may wish to relate a personal experience or one your audience is likely to have had.** Perhaps while leaning back in your lawn chair on some dark night you were suddenly overwhelmed by the vastness of the heavens. All those distant stars and suns seemed to reduce you to an insignificant dot. Or perhaps you have walked along the seashore and observed how the relentless rhythm of the waves erases every footprint. An unanticipated thought

causes you to pause: Will every memory of *my* presence here be swept away like footprints in the sand?

Have you ever had such feelings wash across your soul? In these and other settings our imagination is tickled and our intellect is teased with the most profound questions that can come our way: Where did it all come from? And, more pointedly and personally: Why am I here?

From the pages of history we discover that our feelings and questions are not unique to our century. From the days when people first began to record their thoughts, poets, philosophers, and peasants have asked this fundamental set of questions. And yet, after searching through the stacks in the best university libraries in our world, we realize that life's central questions remain unanswered. Our technological advances have not helped us answer the most crucial and basic concerns of our lives.

1   The Answer in Genesis

A. God, Creation's Creator

Display visual 2A from the CD-ROM here.

The Book of Genesis, written by inspiration of God some 15 hundred years before the birth of Christ by a man called Moses, gives us an answer unlike any other that has been offered. It was a peculiar answer when Moses wrote it. It remains distinctive today.

The very first sentence of Genesis sets it apart: "In the beginning God created the heavens and the earth" (1:1).

Before anything, there was God. Genesis 1:1 does not try to prove this. It simply asserts that not matter, not chaos, not a chorus of gods, but *Elohim* [El-o-HEEM], the one true creator God, existed before everything. The very name *Elohim* in Hebrew carries the impression of majesty and sovereignty over all that is.

Someone making such a claim in Moses' day would have faced the same challenges we meet when we assert it today.

Imagine yourself for the moment at the world's greatest university in Moses' day. This center of learning is located at the heart of a sophisticated society. Ancient Egypt had distinguished itself with previously unequaled achievements in arts and letters as well as in the sciences.

Moses, raised in Pharaoh's court, benefited from the best education Egypt could offer (Exodus 2:10). Unlike most people, Moses enjoyed leisure time to learn the literature and arts of Egypt. As Acts states, he "was educated in all the wisdom of the Egyptians and was powerful in speech and action" (Acts 7:22).

Why, Moses could have gone on a picnic with his palace friends to the Great Pyramid. This structure, already a thousand years old in Moses' day, is proof of Egypt's expertise in mathematics and engineering. The achievements of the Egyptians still astound scientists today! The Egyptian builders worked within margins of error similar to those observed in the construction of modern skyscrapers!

Moses opens his five-volume masterpiece—the Pentateuch—with a simple phrase: *In the beginning.* Moses began with Genesis and then followed with Exodus, Leviticus, Numbers, and Deuteronomy. All five books of the Pentateuch show his interest in mapping the family line of the people of Israel. So serious is Moses' desire to trace Israel's family tree that he takes us back to the beginning of all history!

But why? To answer that, we need to remember that more than the past was on Moses' mind! The children of Israel had spent more than four centuries in Egypt, most of that time as slaves of Egyptians. Egypt had its own explanation of the world. Particularly important to Egyptians was portraying the sun, the stars, and the earthly elements as gods.

Display visual 2B from the CD-ROM here.

By beginning his account of Israel's family tree with the statement that God created "the heavens and the earth," Moses blasts these so-called "gods" off their thrones. The original Hebrew word for "create" is used only with God as the subject and refers to His special, sovereign action. Only the true God, *Elohim,* deserves credit for creating and controlling the universe! Note the word *controlling!*

Display visual 2C from the CD-ROM here.

Chapter 1 stresses God's complete power over His creat-

ing in several ways. First, the text asserts that God simply calls creation into being. His word carries creative, omnipotent power! Moses' contemporaries would have caught the implication. The God of Israel—*not* the Egyptian sun god Re (Ray)—created light. *Elohim* existed before the sun itself. *Elohim* created light that existed before the sun did. Our world is created—the masterpiece, the handiwork of Israel's God!

B. The Good Creation

In Genesis 1 Moses also makes the point that God's creation was good. Over and over (Genesis 1:4, 10, 12, 18, 21, 25) we are told that "God saw that it was good." If this truth seems a bit tedious, perhaps we've only heard the words and missed the point. Moses' contemporaries believed the heavenly bodies were to be feared. Even animals had connections with the hidden forces displayed in the sky.

The good word that Genesis 1 brings to ancient Israel and to us is that "mother nature" is not the home of countless gods. No superstitions! No silly horoscopes! No strange sacrifices! None of these are necessary, because God created the universe. We can give thanks to Him rather than huddling in fear before the forces of the universe!

This adjective *good* evokes more than a lack of fear. It also reminds us of the joy and satisfaction we human creatures receive as we use the things God created. Do you enjoy good food? good music? a good book? a good nap? Genesis 1 says that you need not feel guilty about enjoying these good things. God has given them to you for your pleasure! He Himself took pleasure in their creation, and He wants us—His children—to enjoy them too.

Centuries later a poet of Israel praised God: "He makes grass grow for the cattle, and plants for man to cultivate—bringing forth food from the earth: wine that gladdens the heart of man, oil to make his face shine, and bread that sustains his heart" (Psalm 104:14–15).

The psalmist and Genesis 1 agree that the right response when we view the world is not to make a god of it but to praise its Creator.

Display visual 2D from the CD-ROM here.

C. The Human Center

Another feature on which they agree is that people are the pinnacle of God's creative work. Man and woman are not accidents! They are not incidental! They are at the center of the action! They are the high point of God's creative activity!

Genesis 1 makes this point in two ways. In the literary style of the Old Testament, the last in a series is frequently the most significant. With the creation of man and woman on the sixth day, at the climax of creation, God adds His own comment on human being's central position in the entire universe: *Then God said, "Let Us make man in Our image, in Our likeness, and let them rule over the fish of the sea and the birds of the air, over the livestock, over all the earth, and over all the creatures that move along the ground"* (1:26).

Display visual 2E from the CD-ROM here.

Not only are man and woman the pinnacle of creation, the climax of creation, but we alone are made in the image of God. So rich in meaning is this short phrase that it is difficult to explain fully. This "image of God" includes our imagination and intellect, our souls and spirituality, our place and position in creation. All this is included in the image of God. The image of God did not mean Adam looked like God—God is a spirit, a being with a mind and a will but without a physical body. However, Adam shared God's moral perfection in the beginning. Before the fall into sin, Adam and Eve were sinless. They lived in perfect relationship with God and with one another and with the rest of creation. Perfect love marked these relationships. Above all, that was *very good* (1:31)!

Contrast this with the Egyptian view—the view of Israel's slave masters—that the sun god Re ruled earth and the hoards of insignificant people who swarmed like ants over it. These insignificant humans existed only to serve the pleasure of Re's son, the Pharaoh. Do you see how Genesis 1 would have given the downtrodden children of Israel hope?

Centuries later, King David thought about the wonders of creation. He could not completely understand the wonderful position God had given man and woman in His plan. He wrote:

> When I consider Your heavens, the work of Your fingers, the moon and the stars, which You have set in place, what is man that You are mindful of him, the son of man that You care for him? You made him a little lower than the heavenly beings and crowned him with glory and honor. You made him ruler over the works of Your hands; You put everything under his feet (Psalm 8:3–6).

It is as though David were at the same time reflecting on the heavens and on the primary position of man and woman as described in Genesis 1:26–30.

2   A Peculiar Answer

A. To Moses' Contemporaries

Display visual 2F from the CD-ROM here.

In Moses' world, a world where the mighty armies and the magnificent architecture of Egypt dominated the landscape, Moses' proposal would have seemed peculiar. The great civilizations of that day had their own explanations about how the universe came into being and about the place of humankind in it.

The intricate economies, lavish public works, and unsurpassed prosperity of Egypt and Mesopotamia had seemingly demonstrated beyond reasonable doubt that their explanation of the world's existence were to be believed. It's important to note that in none of them did people play a prominent part. In fact, the existence of man and woman was merely incidental. The real action was with the gods. The most humanity could hope for was to survive.

One of Moses' royal associates might have challenged Genesis 1: "The God of Israel, *Elohim*, who has heard of Him? At most, He would be but one of those lesser, desert deities. Where is His temple? His city? His land?"

Yet, confidently and clearly, Moses makes the claim. Humanity is not the result of a chance contest among the gods. Human beings are the special creation of the one true God. We are made in the very image of this true God—the God who has also *chosen Israel*. Chosen Israel for what? We will get to this in later sessions, but here's a one-sentence summary: God chose Israel to be the nation through whom He would send the world's Messiah, the world's Savior from sin.

B. To Our Own Contemporaries

Has this peculiar perspective of Genesis 1 lost its punch for us? Perhaps we should examine the claims of our contemporaries. Have they come up with better answers than the people of Moses' day?

Display visual 2G from the CD-ROM here.

In our time an excellent representative and articulate spokesman for an alternative answer is the British philosopher Bertrand Russell. This well-known thinker wanted to express his conclusions about the human situation. And he wanted to do it in a way that would get his point across.

After inviting several photojournalists to join him on an excursion boat into the North Sea, Russell waited for the right moment. When the craft crossed the path of a small iceberg, Russell signaled the captain. The crew, previously informed of the philosopher's intent, carefully lowered him onto the little island of ice. From his precarious perch atop the ice, Russell called for the shipboard photographers to snap shots of his position.

Several weeks later, the British, European, and American press prominently featured the philosopher. He had communicated! He had captured the world's attention! More than this, Russell supplied a commentary on the photo, suggesting that it was a parable on his conclusions concerning humanity.

In a word, our condition on planet earth is that of a man on a melting iceberg. With time, Russell added, our sun will grow dim and finally burn out. So the human race will sink into the coldness and darkness of the universe as surely as a lone man will slip from safety into the vastness of the sea. Life is a meaningless journey into nothingness!

It was quite a sermon. Many people believed it. Many people still believe the message and live by it!

Genesis 1 paints precisely the opposite picture of our position in the universe. God arranged all of creation for humanity's welfare and pleasure. He created the universe as a home for His human children! Verse 14: "Let there be lights in the expanse of the sky to separate the day from the night, and let them serve as signs to mark seasons and days and years." Only human creatures count and mark seasons, days, and years! Verse 29: "Then God said, 'I give you every seed-bearing plant on the face of the whole earth and every tree that has fruit with seed in it. They will be yours for food.' " "Yours"? Ours! Fruit trees bear fruit for us! Wheat fields sway in the summer sun for us!

Far from being caught in the meaningless mess of a hostile universe, Genesis 1 positions man and woman at the center of the Creator's good work.

3 The Answer Close Up

The wide-angle view of creation in chapter 1 is followed by the close-up view of the sixth day in chapter 2. Some have imagined an alternative or even contradictory account of creation here. But in reality Moses, inspired by God, simply zeros in to portray a snapshot view that conveys more detail. He doesn't want us to miss the point. Humans are unique in all creation. God's creative plan centers on *us!*

A. Formed by God

The importance of man and woman in God's creative plan could hardly be clearer. Here we see the care with which man is formed in the image of God. Verse 7 of chapter 2: "The LORD God formed the man from the dust of the ground and breathed into his nostrils the breath of life, and the man became a living being." The verb for "form" suggests the work of a potter carefully molding the clay into its final shape (Isaiah 29:16; 44:2).

God's direct involvement is also accented by the act of breathing (2:7) "into his nostrils the breath of life." God's attention to man's needs continues as He provides a place for man to live—a home (2:8): "Now the LORD God had planted a garden in the east, in Eden; and there He put the man He had formed." The beauty of that garden home is difficult to imagine. In verses 9–16, we get a glimpse of the balanced arrangement of its rivers, the splendor of its plants, and the remarkable resources of its setting.

B. Created as Man and Woman

The second chapter of Genesis closes with the creation of woman. The details of this account may be familiar to us, but there is a continuing charm about how God brought man and woman together.

Verse 18, which states, "It is not good for the man to be alone," sets the stage for the creation of woman.

Display visual 2H from the CD-ROM here.

We should not miss the point that people were meant to be with one another. This chapter contradicts the idea that we can be truly happy only when we are not tied down. Adam, when he was completely alone, may have been able to do what he wanted without having to consider someone else, but he lacked that helper he needed. It was not good!

Some have even suggested that Eve's creation as Adam's companion and mate was one more aspect of being created in the image of the triune God. The relationship between these two separate and distinct personalities may well reflect the community of persons within the Godhead itself!

As Adam names the animals (vv. 19–20), the text makes it crystal clear that there was (v. 20) "no suitable helper" for him.

Moses describes God's presentation of Eve to Adam in Scripture's first poem (v. 23). "This," Adam exclaims, is "bone of my bones and flesh of my flesh." These words express great delight. The joy the man and the woman find in one another is immediately linked to the institution of marriage with its primary claim over all other relationships, even those we enjoy with parents (v. 24). The chapter concludes (v. 25) by emphasizing the complete innocence of Adam and Eve.

Adam's maleness and Eve's femaleness belong to God's divine design that they should "become one flesh" (2:24). The fact that they were without clothing *and* without shame is a moving commentary on the good and happy world that God had created *in* them and *for* them.

Conclusion

Perhaps the greatest point that our world has missed in Genesis 1 is the original goodness of God's created universe. In a tragic turn of events—one that Adam and Eve also experienced—human beings today try to exclude God from our use of His good gifts. This omission only twists us into knots.

But before studying that tragic fall in chapter 3, we need to pause and consider. You see, the purity and peace Adam and Eve enjoyed in Eden is not just a long-gone memory, an unrecoverable memory. Christ promises that same peace.

When Jesus directed John the Baptist to His mighty works, there could be no question that *in Jesus* creation was being restored to its pristine purity (Matthew 11:5): "The blind receive sight, the lame walk, those who have leprosy are cured, the deaf hear, the dead are raised, and the good news is preached to the poor."

It is a short step from Adam to Jesus, from Eden to Israel. When we take that step we will be struck by the significance of Genesis 1–2 as we live each day in Christ.

Concluding Activities

Invite participants to read along in their Bibles as the lecture leader reads, slowly and reverently, Psalm 8. Or conclude with a prayer, praising God for His majesty and power. Encourage participants to read the article "Paradise: Before and After" in the enrichment magazine. Then make any necessary announcements and distribute study leaflet 3.

Notes

The Lifeline Is Cut—and Restored

Genesis 3–5

Preparing for the Session

Central Focus

These chapters of Genesis are a study of a good world gone bad. Relationships deteriorate quickly as sin appears and works its way through the world. In these chapters also we find the origin of two kinds of people—one line descended from Cain and the other descended from Seth. They are two branches of the same family tree, both talented. But one, though infected by sin, looks in faith for a Savior, while the other continues on a course of rebellion, arrogance, and violence that moves God to bring down the ax of judgment.

Objectives

That the participant, as a child of God and with the Holy Spirit's help, will be led to

1. recognize God's grace even as the curse of sin falls on the entire human race;

2. understand the God-intended relationships between God, His human creatures, and the world;

3. appreciate the believer's position as a member of God's family and of the line of promise.

Note for small-group leaders: Lesson notes and other materials you will need begin on page 71.

For the Lecture Leader

This week's lecture compares the creation gone awry to the masterpiece of a skilled painter suddenly ruined by one, swift stroke of a paintbrush across the entire canvas. Pray that the Holy Spirit will paint the tragedy of this image on the minds of the listeners—together with the sure and certain hope for restoration through Jesus the Messiah.

Session Plan

Worship

Begin the session with the hymn, devotion, and prayer. The words of the hymn and prayer are printed in the study leaflet. Note that accompaniment for the hymn can be found on the music CD that accompanies this course. If you plan to use it, find it on the disk and cue it up before class.

Devotion

Read Genesis 4:13–16: "Cain said to the LORD, 'My punishment is more than I can bear. Today You are driving me from the land, and I will be hidden from Your presence; I will be a restless wanderer on the earth, and whoever finds me will kill me.' But the LORD said to him, 'Not so; if anyone kills Cain, he will suffer vengeance seven times over.' Then the LORD put a mark on Cain so that no one who found him would kill him. So Cain went out from the LORD'S presence and lived in the land of Nod, east of Eden."

This week we read the familiar story of Cain's murder of his brother Abel. The name *Cain* sounds like the Hebrew for "brought forth" or "acquired." When he was born, Eve declared, "With the help of the LORD I have brought forth a man," an indication she may have believed this child was the promised Seed who would crush the serpent's head (Genesis 3:15). Cain turned out to be anything but that, as he murdered his own brother.

In spite of that, God showed mercy to Cain. We learn about the so-called "mark of Cain" that God graciously used to protect this murderer from his own relatives. Exactly what this mark was, we are not told, but it was effective. Cain lived to establish a family and even build a city.

As believers, you and I also have God's gracious mark on our lives, though we do not deserve it. Even though we might have committed the most wretched crimes imaginable, Christ has paid for all of our sins, protected us with His love, and by His amazing grace has marked us as His holy ones—God's saints.

There is a story about two young brothers who were caught stealing sheep. The punishment back then was to brand the thief's forehead with the letters *S. T.*, which stood for "sheep thief." One brother subsequently left the village and spent his remaining years wandering from place to place, indelibly marked by disgrace. The other remained in the village, made restitution for the stolen sheep, and became a caring friend and neighbor to the townspeople—an old man loved by all. Years later, a stranger came to town and asked about the *S. T.* on the old man's forehead. "I'm not sure what it means," another told him. "It happened so long ago, but I think the letters stand for *saint*."

Indeed, God can change hearts and lives. The fact is that each of us is a sinner and a saint at the same time. Although we sin daily, God forgives us, sets us aside as His own, and marks us with His loving care and protection. Yes, because of what Jesus has done for us, we each wear a mark. In the words of St. Paul, God has "set His seal of ownership on us, and put His Spirit in our hearts" (2 Corinthians 1:22).

Lecture Presentation

This lecture also appears on the CD-ROM that accompanies this course. Also look at the PDFFILES directory on the CD-ROM for visual aids available for the course.

Introduction

The artist had worked deftly for weeks to finish the painting. With a sigh of satisfaction, she stepped back from the canvas. As she withdrew, she marveled, "It is perfect!"

But almost at the same moment, as the brush moved away from the surface, a stray bristle was bent by the movement of the artist's sleeve. The bristle rebounded, flicking small paint spots across the canvas.

The artist was stunned! These tiny spots spoiled the whole painting. And tragically, try as she might, the artist was unable to touch it up to recapture the original perfection. The shift from perfection and pleasure to bitter disappointment had taken but a moment! **You may wish to substitute another illustration closer to the experience of your audience.**

We've all experienced moments that at first held satisfaction but then suddenly and sharply turned to sadness. The athlete who has trained for years and leads the race can inexplicably stumble just a few feet from the finish line!

1 From Perfection to Disaster (3:1–7)

We see in Genesis 2:25 and Genesis 3:1 the same stark contrast. Though they are adjacent verses in the Genesis text, they are worlds apart in tenor and tone. Genesis 2:25 describes perfection; Genesis 3:1 foreshadows imminent disaster!

A. Innocence and Craftiness

Display visual 3A from the CD-ROM here.

The inspired author of Genesis, Moses, captures the perfection of creation—not on canvas—but in the innocence of Adam and Eve. They (2:25) are naked and feel no shame. Like the simplicity of an artistic masterpiece, these words convey the peace of Paradise, the goodness of God's good creation.

The Hebrew text stresses the contrast between Adam and Eve's innocence, *arumim* [a-roo-MIM], in 2:25 and their imminent embarrassment by describing the serpent as crafty, *arum* [a-ROOM], in 3:1. This play on the word *arum* is very similar to what we achieve with the expression *naughty or nice*. There is a great distance between being "naughty" on the one hand and "nice" on the other. There is an even greater distance between the innocence of the two in 2:25 and the craftiness of the one in 3:1. The masterpiece of creation is about to be marred by the serpent, who spits bits of paint onto the divine canvas. This poisonous paint has the power to ruin the masterpiece God had so carefully created.

B. The Serpent

The serpent's character is consistent with his handiwork. If we were asked to describe the craftiness of his character, the third chapter of Genesis provides more than ample proof.

First, this serpent speaks. Since snakes don't speak naturally, who is the agent behind this snake? Could God be responsible, as in the case of Balaam's donkey (Numbers 22)? The answer comes quickly, for the serpent's first words suggest the precise opposite of God's will. God had provided all the trees for food—save one (Genesis 2:16–17). The serpent suggests (3:1) that *all* are forbidden.

The serpent's first speech contains this subtle substitution, but it quickly goes on to forthright contradiction of God's Word. The lie (3:4) "You will not surely die" demonstrates this. This creature lies and calls the Creator a liar! Here is far more than an animal! We are face-to-face with the one whom Revelation 12:9 calls "that ancient serpent," who is rightly recognized as our opponent—Satan.

The subtlety of his approach to Eve includes his appeal (Genesis 3:6) to the attractiveness of the tree and his (vv. 5–6) false promise that such eating would make Eve "like God."

C. The Woman's Seed

Who will oppose this one who has so slyly moved Adam and Eve from innocence to shame (2:25 and 3:7), from communion with God (2:15–18) to painful embarrassment at His presence (3:7)?

Display visual 3B from the CD-ROM here.

God first confines the serpent with a curse (3:14). Then in Scripture's first promise of the Savior, God sets against Satan the "offspring" of the woman (3:15): "I will put enmity between you and the woman, and between your offspring and hers; He will crush your head, and you will strike His heel." Hatred ("enmity") will mark Satan's relationship between God's human creatures and Satan. Satan hates God. He hates God's people.

Display visual 3C from the CD-ROM here.

He especially hated the Savior, the "offspring," or Seed, whom God would send. Satan would strike out at Christ again and again during His earthly life and would finally—on the cross—strike His heel.

Display visual 3D from the CD-ROM here.

Yet, death would not hold this Holy One, the Seed of the woman. In rising again to life, Jesus would forever crush the head of the serpent (Galatians 4:4; 1 John 3:8).

God quickly and mercifully offers this promise to Adam and Eve in their darkest moment. The perfection of God's good creation had been penetrated by the poisonous power of pride. Yet paradise would one day be restored in Jesus—the second Adam who would fully obey the Law of the Creator, the Law (Romans 5:18–21) the first Adam broke.

D. The Problem of Pride

Display visual 3E from the CD-ROM here.

Indeed, so sad is the scene in Genesis 3 that generations of believers have puzzled over how God could have permitted His masterpiece to be mutilated in such a manner. Why was it necessary to have the tree of the knowledge of good and evil in the garden? Where did such an evil agent as the snake come from? What could have possessed Adam and Eve to violate this one prohibition? While there is finally a mystery about the fall into sin that will escape our complete understanding, it is still helpful to reflect on what happened. The consequences are so catastrophic! It is natural to ask what caused this condition!

As we ponder this mystery, perhaps an example will help us begin to understand it. Do you recall when you were a teenager? Do you presently have a teenager at home? Or do you know of someone who does? **A personal reference may be appropriate here. Most of us are familiar with that delicate period that comes before independence and adulthood. Most of us would probably also suggest that there is a time when parents must permit young adults to have their own will.**

As painful as it can be, parental love finally risks even rejection. To program or pressure our offspring to the point where they lose their own will would, for the

Christian parent, be wrong. We want our children to become responsible adults, not robots. That's what God wanted too. He did not program Adam and Eve for rigid obedience that permitted only zombielike compliance. No, in a remarkable extension of His grace, He created Adam and Eve with their own will! They could freely love and obey Him. But that freedom opened another possibility. They could freely reject His love and disobey as well. That's what freedom means. At times when our own sin and the sin of others bring pain into our lives we sometimes second-guess God. Might we have been better off as robots? But such thoughts grow out of sinful, prideful hearts, hearts that accuse God—along with Eve and Adam. Could our Creator be holding out on us? Could He deny us the best things, giving us only second-best gifts?

You know the answer to that. You've seen the answer to that in Jesus, who hung and bled and died for you on a gory cross. God is not a withholder. Yet, our prideful hearts want to believe we know better than He what's good for us.

If we're perfectly honest with ourselves, isn't our pride the most vulnerable point in our makeup? When that voice from within calls for us to act in a way that is not in harmony with our Baptism, to follow *our own* preferences or insights, isn't there a precise parallel to aspects of Adam's fall?

Pride is that ugly paint splattered across God's masterpiece! Pride still prevents people from hearing God's promise of mercy in the woman's Offspring (Seed)!

2 Consequences of the Fall

Genesis 3, furthermore, portrays how pervasive were the consequences of the fall. No section of the canvas escaped the damage.

A. Relationship with God

Display visual 3F from the CD-ROM here.

Immediately evident is the break of Adam and Eve's relationship with God. An ancient rabbi wryly comments that when God asked Adam, "Where are you?" (3:9), the point is not that *God* didn't know where Adam was, but that *Adam* no longer knew where he was!

Adam's awful admission "I was afraid" (3:10) says it all! From this time on, fear would mark man and woman's relationship to their Maker.

B. Man and Woman

As a result of this broken relationship with God, there was also a break in the relationship between Adam and Eve. The natural delight they had taken in one another, which was part of them in chapter 2, is turned into tension and strife. Instead of accepting responsibility for his disobedience, Adam accuses Eve (3:12)—and God Himself ("the woman You put here with me"). Eve, in turn, points at the serpent (3:13). The pleasant spontaneity of Adam's relationship with Eve (Genesis 2:23) is replaced by the power structure of Genesis 3:16. We see the struggle for mastery, for control, for having the last word in marriages still today.

C. Creation and Creature

The final rift the fall into sin brought about was that between creation and its creatures. Now childbearing would involve (3:16) painful labor, and growing food from the ground would require (3:17) painful toil.

As a famous photographer of nature commented: "Along with the smile of its beauty, the face of mother nature can display a sudden ferocity. The remoteness of a wilderness or the mountains in winter represent a beauty that can bring death to the poorly prepared."

D. God's Response

So, the fall has brought fear: fear of God, fear of others, fear of the natural, created world. Is it surprising then that the Second Adam, the Offspring of woman (3:15), would frequently invite those of faith to "not be afraid" (Matthew 28:10)?

Jesus came to conquer our fears. This same faith in God's deliverance can be seen in Eve's exclamation in Genesis 4:1 when she describes the birth of Cain: "I have the man, the Lord" (the translation of Martin Luther and the literal reading of the Hebrew text). In Eve's words we read the truth that she and Adam had understood the promise of 3:15, God's promise of a Savior. Eve clung to that promise by faith. In fact, some have read into her words the understanding that her newborn son was that Savior. Cain's terrible life history shows he wasn't, but still if we read Eve's exclamation with that understanding, we see both her longing for God's promised salvation and her Spirit-given confidence that God would one day grant it. Already Eve sees that only faith in God's gracious promise can overcome the multiple fears that the fall brought about in the human heart.

Genesis 3:21–24 continues to reveal that God's disposition toward Adam and Eve, even after the fall, was not hateful or vindictive. The God who had clothed all of creation with power and glory (Psalm 8) now bends down (Genesis 3:21) to become a tailor for Adam and Eve. The Father's attentive care in fashioning garments dispelled the fear and shame that had caused our first parents to flee from Him. In this act of kindness we also see Christ's death foreshadowed. Adam and Eve should have died. And yet God "sacrificed" animals in their place and covered His children's shame with the animal hides. One day another Substitute would die in naked disgrace, bearing the punishment all sinners had deserved. So deep is the heavenly Father's compassion. Yet, even as God's presence and promise bring hope to Adam and Eve, the consequences of the fall become more evident.

3 Two Lines

Display visual 3G from the CD-ROM here.

After the initial enthusiasm surrounding Cain's birth, Genesis 4 records the truth that disobedience would bring death. Cain (4:8) kills Abel. Again, God probes the sinner's heart with a question (4:9): "Where is your brother Abel?" Cain's deceptive reply sounds a lot like his father's dodge in Eden. It also reveals something of Cain's disrespect for his Creator. Cain says in essence (4:9), "How should I know? Nobody put me in charge of his well-being." Cain's ungodly attitude and violent nature continued as by nature and by example he passed them down to his children and his children's children. The climax came (vv. 17–24) with Lamech's boast to his two wives that he too, like Cain, has slain a young man.

But the ungodly line of Cain is not the only family on earth. In (4:25) the birth of Seth, God gives Adam and Eve relief and hope. Cain's line promises only death! But God gives Seth (4:25) to replace Abel. His family begins to "call on the name of the LORD" (4:26), to worship and to look to Him for mercy and for pardon.

Genesis 5 continues the contrast between death and life, between despair and hope. If most genealogies make for dull reading, few of us can resist the record of our own ancestors. How fascinating to follow each generation as it wends its way toward us! Genesis 5 records our common ancestry. From Adam to Noah, from the creation to the flood, we are of one blood.

Two features of our genealogy are particularly noteworthy. First, the tragic refrain "he lived … and he died" tolls like a funeral bell throughout this chapter. Again and again we see the truth: The wages of sin is death. The chapter holds the harsh truth before us. All humanity was delivered up to death in Adam's prideful rebellion. And yet, a glimmer of hope shines out from this darkness— the hope of the birth that would reverse the serpent's curse. As long as the line goes on, the woman's Offspring, the Seed, can come! The head of Satan can be crushed! Even death need not have the final word! Such a hope is affirmed in Enoch: "Enoch walked with God; then he was no more, because God took him away" (5:24).

Conclusion

So the sequence of events in Genesis 3–5 has instructed us about a great deal more than the history of a distant past! What we have perceived, if we've not missed the point, is that these events have shaped us and our world. They have left us with the present reality of physical death that even medical science cannot overcome. *Our* world, *our* humanity, and *our* pride are described in this text. It explains the present as it describes the past.

And the hope that shines from these pages lights up our hearts too. The woman's Offspring, the Seed who was to come, has now accomplished what God sent Him to do. In Jesus of Nazareth, the Son of Mary, the promise is kept. The curse is reversed. In Jesus, death loses its sting. In Jesus, we have become children of the heavenly Father and heirs of eternal life. In Jesus, we lose our terror and receive the freedom to worship our Creator in wonder and awe.

Concluding Activities

Conclude by reading, or having someone read, Psalm 32 while the others follow in their Bibles. Then speak a brief prayer, thanking God for forgiveness through Jesus. Encourage participants to read the articles "Face-to-Face with Your Maker" and "Genesis in the Lab" in the enrichment magazine. Distribute study leaflet 4 after making any necessary announcements.

Notes

The Lifeline Is Narrowed

Genesis 6–10

Preparing for the Session

Central Focus

The study of Noah and the ark is one of the Bible's definitive examples of how God can be just and merciful at the same time. Although our natural curiosity makes it tempting to dwell on the catastrophic elements of the flood account, the most important aspect of this story is how God lovingly and patiently protects a righteous remnant so that the lifeline to a Messiah can continue.

Objectives

That the participant, as a child of God and with the Holy Spirit's help, will be led to

1. understand that God must punish sin;

2. rejoice in God's patience in dealing with sinners;

3. see God's covenant protection in our lives today;

4. discover the genealogical roots of our civilization.

Note for small-group leaders: Lesson notes and other materials you will need begin on page 74.

For the Lecture Leader

In studying the great flood, students (and leaders) might easily lose sight of the forest while looking at individual trees. Questions about the exact size and shape of the ark, how many animals it contained, where all the water came from, and how it disappeared are worthy of discussion—but not at the expense of time spent in appreciating God's patience in dealing with thoroughly evil people and how God's covenant love demonstrated itself toward Noah and his family.

Be aware that the lecture for this session presents a picture of God's grace in the midst of God's judgment, of a God who not only brings a flood but also an ark and a rainbow. In spite of man's utter corruption, the Lord is still willing to sáve a vestige of humanity for the sake of future generations who will come to know the Messiah. Your goal will be to lead the hearer into a greater appreciation of God's grace that comes to us still today through the waters of Holy Baptism. (Note: The devotional opening is longer and the lecture is shorter than usual. To compensate, you may want to begin the small-group discussion period five minutes later and end it five minutes later.)

Session Plan

Worship

Begin the session with the hymn, devotion, and prayer. The words of the hymn and prayer are printed in the study leaflet. Note that accompaniment for the hymn can be found on the music CD that accompanies this course. If you plan to use it, find it on the disk and cue it up before class.

Devotion

Read Genesis 8:22: "As long as the earth endures, seedtime and harvest, cold and heat, summer and winter, day and night will never cease."

Promises. Promises. Life is filled with promises. Contracts, marriages, hopes and dreams, love and faith—so much depends on promises.

Following the great flood, in which all but one family had been destroyed, Noah and his family left the ark. It had been about a year since Noah had been on dry land, and the first thing we hear of him doing after leaving the ark is that he built an altar and made a sacrifice to God. Then God made a twofold promise—He would never again destroy the world with a flood, and He would continue to provide the seasons and life-giving crops.

What a tremendous promise this is! As long as the world lasts, there will be seasons for planting and harvesting. God says He will provide for life on earth. From this promise we can learn a number of lessons. One is that God is reliable. During the hundreds, the thousands, of years since Noah and his family left the ark, God has never failed to bless the earth with crops to sustain life. This alone ought to be enough to lead us to do as Jesus has commanded us: trust in God to provide and not worry about tomorrow. And is it not a special reminder to us of how thankful we can be that God not only provides for us, but that He does so richly and daily? In spite of our complaining about rising costs and financial shortfalls, we still have been blessed by God beyond measure when it comes to those gifts that preserve our lives on earth.

This promise is only one among many promises of our Creator. In addition to His promise to meet our physical needs, He promises help in hard times and in sickness. He promises that brighter days will always follow dark days. He promises to answer all of our prayers. God promises strength to resist temptation. And, in Christ, He promises the forgiveness of sins and eternal life in heaven. In His love, God even promises that He will work *everything* together for our good.

These are but some of God's priceless promises. Not only does God make such promises—but He also declares that they never have been and never will be broken. Nor has any promise God has made ever failed to come true. Is this not reason enough to thank God? He has promised us everything that we need and more than we could ever ask for.

Lecture Presentation

This lecture also appears on the CD-ROM that accompanies this course. Also look at the PDFFILES directory on the CD-ROM for visual aids available for the course.

Introduction

Hiroshima. Nagasaki. What comes to mind when you hear those words?

For many, these Japanese cities symbolize the nuclear age. It was toward Hiroshima that a solitary bomber

headed on the morning of August 6, 1945. By that evening a single bomb had reduced the entire city to rubble. The half-million hustling inhabitants lost their lives in a roar of destruction that took but a few moments. Three days later Nagasaki met the same fate.

These two events changed the world—not just for the tragic victims but for everyone, all of us. These cities present a watershed in human history. All of us now know that, in but a few moments, the glories of our greatest cities can be ground to dust by the might of nuclear arms! Never again can we feel the same sense of security that was possible. The world is simply a different place than it was before Hiroshima and Nagasaki.

Genesis 6–9 describes an event similar in its importance. The events of these chapters changed the course of history! The world and the place of humans in it would never be the same again. In fact, just as the awful mushroom clouds of those nuclear explosions still today cast a shadow over our world, so the rainbow that follows the storm clouds today reminds us of another disaster long ago. The mushroom cloud warns us of what *could* happen. The rainbow symbolizes a divine promise that what *did* happen will *not* happen again.

1 The Human Condition: Sinful Rebellion

As we turn to the opening verses of Genesis 6, a troubled mood alerts the reader that something extraordinary—something that will change all that follows—is about to occur. On the surface the scene seems normal, like a city before a catastrophe (6:1): "When men began to increase in number on the earth and daughters were born to them …" Everything appears normal. God had commanded that humanity multiply (1:28). The scene, if anything, is marked by a certain orderliness.

Display visual 4A from the CD-ROM here.

The promise of a Savior, the Offspring, or Seed (3:15), the replacement of Abel with Seth (4:25), and the lengthy genealogy of Genesis 5 combine to confirm God's design in sustaining the line of life. While God's human creatures may resort to violence (Genesis 4) and death may reap each generation's elderly (Genesis 5), the family line continues in accord with God's direction.

A. Imminent Disaster

So all seems as it should be in Genesis 6:1. But in verse 2, the bomb falls: "The sons of God saw that the daughters of men were beautiful, and they married any of them they chose." Several explanations have been offered for these words. It's most likely that they refer to the line of believers (Seth) intermarrying with unbelievers (the descendants of Cain). The indecency of these marriages is indicated by God's displeasure in verse 3: "The LORD said, 'My Spirit will not contend with man forever, for he is mortal; his days will be a hundred and twenty years.' "

This further insults the Lord's plan for humanity. The good world of Genesis 1–2 has been reduced to rubble. Sin has spoiled everything. The scene is tragic, for God's Spirit had sought to remain with the line of Seth. His family had begun to "call on the name of the LORD" in formal worship (4:26). God's attentiveness to Seth's family ("the sons of God") was helped along by the long lives of its members (Genesis 5) and the opportunities their longevity gave for witnessing to each new generation. Yet, just like Adam and Eve, the children of Seth follow their own will rather than the will of God's Spirit. Their desire to marry any they chose (6:2) incites another prideful rebellion. Not God's will, but their own sinful will would finally determine how they would live.

Finally, God's patience runs out! By embracing the daughters—and the values—of the line of Cain (Genesis 4), the "sons of God" had rejected the Spirit of God (6:3). This rejection also brought a reduction in the human life span. God's grace would no longer fall for centuries on such pride.

The consequences of this latest rebellion appeared quickly (6:5): "The LORD saw how great man's wickedness on the earth had become, and that every inclination of the thoughts of his heart was only evil all the time." What this text stresses can scarcely be missed. "Every inclination" is evil! "Only evil" is on the mind "all the time!" The pride that had caused Adam and Eve to attempt to be like God has now paraded itself in public. So (v. 7) God resolves to end such an evil order. His remarkable act of love in granting Adam and Eve the gift of free will has not brought a spontaneous embrace of God's Spirit, but instead only a willful and prideful rejection of the gracious heavenly Father.

B. God's Favor

But now, into this world tottering on the very brink of complete destruction, comes God's gracious favor. God's favor rests on one man: Noah. In Noah this favor is not wasted. God's favor produces fruit: "Noah was a righteous man, blameless among the people of his time, and he walked with God" (6:9).

Noah, like Enoch (5:24), stood out in the crowds. His life would be shaped by different standards. God's gracious favor would lead him to walk a different route.

This contrast between the many and the one, between the masses and the man sets the stage for the flood. It also alerts us: Majority opinion is not necessarily trustworthy (Matthew 7:13–14). In fact, the majority provoke God's judgment. The divine gaze falls on a sorry sight (6:12): "God saw how corrupt the earth had become, for all the people on earth had corrupted their ways." The repetition of this idea underscores the sorry state of "all the people."

But what about that? Wasn't Noah caught in sin like the rest of fallen humanity? Certainly. Noah and his family inherited Adam's sin just as we all have. Noah deserved eternal destruction just as we all do. Yet Hebrews 11:7 tells us how he escaped it: "By faith Noah … in holy fear built an ark to save his family." Noah was counted righteous, just as you and I are counted righteous—by God's grace through faith in one who died for all human rebellion.

Display visual 4B from CD-ROM here.

"In holy fear [Noah] built an ark." May God work that same holy fear in our hearts as we grieve over the senseless violence and rebellion we see in the culture all around us. May we, by grace, stand out like lights as we shine in this dark world, holding out the hope of Christ to sinners all around us!

God, in grace, did not forget Noah. Just as He fashioned garments for Adam and Eve (3:21), so now He will provide specific deliverance for Noah. Noah (6:14) is to build a great boat so that his household might survive.

The divinely dictated dimensions are 450 feet by 75 feet by 45 feet—proportions very close to those of modern supertankers.

We should note that the only other use of the word for "ark" in the Bible is for the watertight "basket" in which (Exodus 2:3) the infant Moses floated to rescue on the Nile. When early Christians viewed the church as God's ark to carry them through this life to heaven, they were using a meaningful word picture. God was gracious to Noah. He is likewise gracious to us, providing in our church a place of safety and peace despite the darkness and the deluge of sin that is even now destroying those who reject God's gracious Gospel call.

2 The Great Flood

Just as Genesis 6:1–13 contrasts the population at large with Noah, God's deeds mirror this division. On one hand (Genesis 6:17), "all life" and "every creature that has the breath of life" will perish. On the other hand (6:18), God will establish His saving covenant with Noah. This covenant is a personal pact placing Noah in a particular position. He and his household are to receive God's favor. As we have seen, Noah's receptivity to God's favor is rightly described as faith (Hebrews 11:7) and it is God's gift to Noah: "By faith Noah, when warned about things not yet seen, in holy fear built an ark to save his family." The response of faith to such favor is action (Genesis 6:22): "Noah did everything just as God commanded him."

Our curiosity can easily lead us away from this focus on God's favor and Noah's faith. When did the flood occur? From where did the vast amounts of water come? How did it change the face of the earth? These are tantalizing questions. Scientists continue to debate whether the current theories concerning the earth's history are compatible with such a flood. And yet, fascinating as these questions are to us, the text focuses our attention on another arena. Noah and his family (7:1) have received God's favor! God's gracious covenant will protect them even in this catastrophe.

This fact is even more remarkable than the flood! *Elohim*—the God who created all that is—can command creation as He wishes. A worldwide flood is a small matter for the Creator of the entire universe. The text goes beyond asserting God's power to underscore in a number of ways the extraordinary grace of God in the face of such human wickedness!

How does the text make this point? The most obvious way is by describing Noah's deliverance in the ark (7:6–8:19). All are lost! Only those in the ark are spared! However, other features of the text speak eloquently of God's saving action. Note, for example, how (7:15) "pairs of all creatures that have the breath of life in them came to Noah and entered the ark." Noah and his family will witness the way things were to be. Without the fall, the animals and all of creation would have served man on their own. The sight of all the animals willingly streaming, two by two, toward the ark recalls the good order of God's good creation in Genesis 1. It is also significant (7:16) that God Himself shuts Noah in. The hand of God would secure the door so that Noah would be safe!

The contrast between the wickedness of the world and the righteousness of Noah in Genesis 6 is paralleled in the description of the flood's consequences at the end of chapter 7. Every living thing was destroyed; man and animals—all the creatures that move along the ground and all the birds of the air—were wiped from the face of the earth. Only Noah and those with him in the ark remained. Since the thoughts of mankind were (6:5) "only evil," (7:23) "only" Noah would survive.

3 The Favored Line: Slender but Strong

Noah would do more than survive! God would (8:1) "remember" him! This remembrance brings blessings (Genesis 19:29; Exodus 2:24). The waters (8:1–14) recede. The invitation (8:15–17) to "come out" comes directly from God to Noah.

Display visual 4C from CD-ROM here.

All the pleasant details of God's covenant are spelled out in Genesis 9. Noah's family will live under the same blessing (Genesis 1:28; 9:1) that Adam's family had enjoyed.

Food is provided not only from the plant world (1:29–30), but also (9:3) from the animal world. The life of each human being will be protected by divine prohibition from the violence (9:6) that had characterized the world before the flood.

God graciously promises (9:11–16) that never again will a flood destroy the world. The rainbow's beauty (9:17) serves as sign and summary of a whole package of blessings that this covenant bestows. The remarkably gracious character of God is displayed in the lavish blessings of this covenant. God does not stand far off from His human creatures; in detail after detail we see how He tends to Noah's needs.

At the same time, Noah's character takes on concrete contours. On the positive side, he trusts God's promises even when appearances point the other way. As he built his great boat, he must have looked laughable to the general public! It's not hard to imagine the sneers and jeers such a project would generate. The intellectuals and the masses alike must have thought it all very funny. But Noah's faith stands firm! God's favor—His grace—sustained that faith.

Still, we see evidence that Noah sprang from Adam's family tree. We learn (9:21) that Noah became drunk. As so frequently happens, one sin quickly spawns a whole series. Ham (v. 22) ridicules his father's condition and tells his brothers. Noah responds (9:25) by cursing Canaan, Ham's son. No one knows why Noah directed this curse at Canaan rather than at Ham. Perhaps he had not yet sobered up. At any rate, we see in graphic detail that Noah needed a Savior just as much as any one of us.

Genesis 10 charts the consequences of all this for the human family. Ham, Shem, and Japheth will father all earth's nations. God's determination that the Seed (or Offspring) of the woman will reverse the consequences and curses of sin, whether Adam's, Noah's, or Ham's, can be seen in the blessing upon Shem (9:26) and in the position of Shem's line in Genesis 10. As in Genesis 5, that line bearing the promise of the woman's Seed, the Messiah, is placed last (10:21–32).

God's promise is sure. He will bring it about though the whole world be washed away! He will keep His promises though all humanity be caught in its own excesses. God's favor (7:1) will rest on those who by faith have received His gift of righteousness.

Seen in this light, Genesis 6–10 is as much about God's grace as it is about God's wrath. The flood does consume the prideful rebellion of humanity. But the focus of the text is upon God's favor. He provides an ark. This special vessel bobbing over the vast waters shows that God's promise can be trusted.

Conclusion

It is no accident that Jesus urges us to focus our faith on His sure promise rather than on the fickle opinions of the general population (Matthew 24:37–39): "As it was in the days of Noah, so it will be at the coming of the Son of Man. For in the days before the flood, people were eating and drinking, marrying and giving in marriage, up to the day Noah entered the ark; and they knew nothing about what would happen until the flood came and took them all away. That is how it will be at the coming of the Son of Man." The contrast between the evil inclination of humanity and the saving intent of God's promise marked Noah's generation. It marked Jesus' generation. It also marks ours.

May Noah's faith, despite the wickedness of a sinful world, serve as a model for us. But far more importantly, may God's free promise of grace and mercy in the Seed of the woman refresh and renew us. Jesus' coming in the flesh gives us much cause to celebrate. His ascension into the heavens gives us reason to wait for His return. God's favor in Christ makes us safe.

Concluding Activities

Read Psalm 1 or Matthew 7:24–27, perhaps in unison. Then thank God for providing the means of our eternal deliverance in Jesus. After making any necessary announcements, distribute study leaflet 5 and encourage participants to read the article "The Flood" in the enrichment magazine.

Notes

The Lifeline Is Strengthened

Genesis 11–13

Preparing for the Session

Central Focus

Just as God saved Noah even while He executed judgment on sinful mankind, so God in His mercy called Abram from a world of proud pagans to carry on the line of promise.

Objectives

That the participant, as a child of God and with the Holy Spirit's help, will be led to

1. recognize the reasons for God's judgment on a world that sees no need for the true God;

2. praise God for His mercy showered on the world through the call of Abram;

3. rely on God's forgiveness through the world's Savior just as Abram did—by grace;

4. learn that through Abram's Descendant—Jesus— we also have been blessed to be a blessing.

Note for small-group leaders: Lesson notes and other materials you will need begin on page 77.

For the Lecture Leader

Again, the devotional opening is longer than usual and the lecture shorter than usual. You may therefore wish to announce a five-minute longer opening devotion, counterbalanced by a five-minute later than usual ending for the discussion period.

Session Plan

Worship

Begin the session with the hymn, devotion, and prayer. The words of the hymn and prayer are printed in the study leaflet. Note that accompaniment for the hymn can be found on the music CD that accompanies this course. If you plan to use it, find it on the disk and cue it up before class.

Devotion

A young transient was looking for odd jobs to earn spending money. He knocked on the side door of a large, expensive-looking house. The owner was in an amiable mood, so she told the young man to paint the porch, using the green paint in the garage. A few hours later, the young man—covered with green paint from head to toe—returned for his pay. As he pocketed the $50 he said, "By the way, ma'am, that's not a Porsche, it's a Ferrari."

Just because we send a message to another person does not necessarily mean we have communicated! Misunderstandings can lead to difficulty or even disaster. The Scandinavian communications expert, Osmo Wiio has concluded, "If communication can fail it will fail. If it cannot fail, it still will fail."

In whatever language, the major challenge of communication is making yourself understood. H. Norman Wright, a well-known Christian marriage counselor, both explained and demonstrated the problem in the following sentence: "I know you believe you understand what you think I said, but I'm not sure you realize that what you heard is not what I meant."

Adam and Eve understood very clearly what God meant in Eden. They simply chose to ignore His command. By the time God unleashed the great flood upon the earth, communication had truly failed—so much so, that only Noah's immediate family understood and believed the severity of God's words.

After the flood, communication should have succeeded. Everyone spoke the same language. God had given the human race a second chance to fill the whole earth. But the spores of human pride that survived the floodwaters germinated in the hearts of arrogant, rebellious people. Cloistering themselves within the walls of a renowned city, they attempted to build a tower "reaching into the heavens." Apparently they were dabbling in the occult, trying to determine their own destiny instead of worshiping and obeying the one true God. This time God graciously chose to disperse them rather than to immerse them once again.

Do we hear and understand God's will any better today? Do we always hear the Word of God and obey it? Hardly. We often choose to ignore our Lord's commands. Even so, God wanted to communicate clearly the love He has for us. To do that, He didn't send us a letter. He sent us His Son, the Word Incarnate. Obeying God in our place, He kept the Law perfectly. Loving us with infinite love, He carried our sins to Calvary's cross to pay the penalty we should have paid. Now our Savior unties our tongues to sing God's praises and to speak the Word of life to others. He is the one who makes us fluent enough to be heard over the babble of the world's false religions. God grant us, then, a thousand voices to sing the sweet song of salvation—to sing it in a tongue that transcends national boundaries and every cultural and language barrier!

Lecture Presentation

This lecture also appears on the CD-ROM that accompanies this course. Also look at the PDFFILES directory on the CD-ROM for visual aids available for the course.

Introduction

You may begin the lecture with a personal experience something like the one described in the first paragraph. Have you ever traveled in a foreign country or listened to a radio or TV broadcast in a foreign language? It can be fun when others smile and clearly enjoy our first efforts to speak in their native tongue. It can also be frustrating when you think you've ordered ice cream and the waiter brings you mashed potatoes. We tend to take language for granted until we find ourselves in a

setting where *our* language is the "foreign language"!

The first 11 chapters of Genesis highlight the importance of language in God's created order. In Genesis 1 God calls everything into existence by simply speaking. He repeatedly (1:31) pronounces that creation good. The bright light that language can cast over all creation is capsulized in God's blessings, spoken over (1:28) man and woman, over (9:1) Noah and his family, and over (9:26) the line of Shem. We see the dark side of language in the curses on the serpent (3:14), the land (3:17), Cain (4:11), and Canaan (9:25).

This week Genesis 11 calls our attention to the crucial place of language in the human family. It particularly points to the tongue as a key indicator of the condition of the heart. A very short step separates Genesis from St. James's admonition (James 3:10): "Out of the same mouth come praise and cursing. My brothers, this should not be."

How do we use *our* lips and *our* language? The answer to this question, whether in ancient Babylon or in a modern metropolis, reveals what lies in our heart (Mark 7:20–23).

Genesis 11:1 illustrates the harmony that having only one language can bring to the human community. While Noah's descendants had developed their own dialects (10:5, 20, 31), a common language still made communication natural and universal. The question that Genesis 11 immediately poses is whether human beings will use this good gift from God as a blessing or turn it into a curse.

1 Towers and Theology: The Use of Language

Genesis 1–3 stresses the unity of humanity. A common language helps the people build the cities in the plain of Shinar. The reference to improved technical skills (11:3) suggests some interesting archaeological associations. The archaeologist's spade has uncovered in the ancient Sumerian city of Ur a sprawling complex of temple buildings dating from approximately 2500 B.C. We know that Ur was the home of Abram's family (Genesis 11:31).

Display visual 5A from the CD-ROM here.

Local pride in this complex clearly shows in its massive temple tower. This expansive structure, known as a ziggurat, was expertly designed and skillfully built. It rose some six stories over the plain of Shinar, the very place where Genesis 11 locates these events. While there is not enough evidence to suggest this structure is related to the one described in Genesis 11, its advanced technology and comparable features are evident. Refinements in the process of making bricks (11:3) had made it possible to build on grander scales than ever before.

Another significant feature uncovered by archaeologists is the central place the tower, or ziggurat, played in the religious and public life of ancient Sumer. The great tower was thought to be a direct route to the home of the gods. These tower and temple complexes became the hubs around which all of life in Sumer revolved. Records for food and beverage provision from this early date indicate that one such complex had no fewer than 1,200 people in its immediate service. A farmer in the fields of ancient Sumer could be assured of the moon god's protection by looking up from the desert and gazing at the great ziggurat of Nanna—the moon god— from as far as 20 miles away. Its height and size dominated the plain of Shinar.

So the cultural and social setting of Genesis 11 is consistent with our earliest, recoverable evidence concerning the world's oldest civilization at ancient Sumer. But, of course, Genesis 11 directs our attention away from these ancient achievements to the terrible purpose toward which this technology and common language were directed. The tower was intended as a prideful rebellion against the true God.

Display visual 5B from the CD-ROM here.

The parallels with Genesis 3 are very close. In Genesis 3:5, the serpent had promised Adam and Eve would be "like God." In Genesis 11:4 the people sought to build "a city, with a tower that reaches to the heavens." In ancient times the heavens were identified with God's being and presence. Just as Adam and Eve reached for the forbidden fruit, so now their descendants reached up toward the heavens. The pride of earth's first parents is now reflected in the pride of a whole generation of their children.

The word *Babel* summarizes this episode. In the ancient Akkadian language (spoken in Babylon) *Babel* means "gateway to a god." In Hebrew the same basic word means "to confuse." When people sought to enter the divine realm through a gateway of their own construction, there was nothing "divine" about the consequences. Complete and utter confusion (11:7) resulted! No longer could people understand one another.

Just as God (3:23–24) had separated Adam and Eve from the Garden of Eden, so now humanity (11:9) is scattered across the face of the earth. What God had given—a good garden and a common language—were now both lost! To live in a peaceful community where mutual understanding prevailed would now be more difficult. The language barrier would join other obstacles separating human beings into conflicting camps. This event simply and truthfully explains the mysterious origin of distinct languages on earth, a mystery that still puzzles anthropologists.

The conspiracy hatched against God in Genesis 11 brought separation from God and from others. Here again, we see the pattern of Genesis 3 repeated. Sin brings separation—separation from God and separation from fellow human beings. True community and oneness will only be restored in Eve's promised Offspring, that Seed of the woman, whose cross will bridge the chasm that human sin created.

Genesis 11:10–32 focuses our attention on this fact. This genealogy points us once again to the lifeline, to the line of Shem, to the messianic line. Only in this line can we hope to experience oneness with God and with one another! Again, the genealogies, so uninteresting to contemporary minds, actually carry the key message for the biblical authors (Matthew 1; Luke 3). The line of Shem stands in sharp contrast to the rest of humanity. Here we read of how God's good hand guided Shem's line toward a marvelous moment. The generations in this genealogy lead us (11:29) to Abram and his wife, Sarai. They are located (11:31) first at Ur and then at Haran.

Display visual 5C from the CD-ROM here.

All this movement, through many generations and across the many miles of the major trade route from Ur to Haran, brings us to one of the key moments in all biblical history. The Lord comes to Abram with a command (12:1): "Leave your country, your people and your father's household and go to the land I will show you."

This command may not impress us as particularly difficult. We are accustomed to children departing for college and for careers in far-off places. In Abram's world the impression would have been very different. The only social unit that really mattered was the extended family. Almost without exception a person's whole life was lived with cousins, uncles, parents, and grandparents. All that was needed for life—food, protection, and so on—was tied to family. Yet God urges Abram to leave such security for a "land I will show you." Then (12:2–3) the Lord connects His command to a series of promises: "I will make you into a great nation ... I will bless you; I will make your name great ... I will bless those who bless you, and whoever curses you I will curse."

2 Abram's Faith

What is remarkable is that Abram responds immediately! Genesis 12:4 tells us, "So Abram left, as the LORD had told him." Abram travels (12:5) to Canaan. There the Lord appears to him with another promise (12:7–8): this land will belong to Abram's children. Abram responds in spontaneous worship. Both in his going and in his giving of thanks, Abram displays complete trust in the Lord's promise—a trust worked by God's Spirit through the word of promise He had given.

From an objective point of view, there were serious reasons for Abram to have doubted. These promises appear so grandiose! The Canaanites were, after all, well established in the land. They had fortified cities and standing armies. They had seen nomadic figures like Abram come and go! Yet, God had promised. Abram believed. And Abram acted on that belief!

3 Abram's Family

At the same time, we need to remember that Abram comes from Adam's line. We see (12:1–8) his faith at

one moment and his frailty (12:9–20) the next. By faith, Abram was prepared to leave everything for God's promise. But in doubt Abram acted on his fear that God would not or could not provide.

Abram's fear (12:12) is focused on Sarai. Perhaps the Egyptians will kill him to lay hold of his beautiful wife! From a human point of view, that fear was well-founded. Ancient kings would commonly kill a husband to add a particularly beautiful woman to their harem. This search for beauty is demonstrated (12:14–15) by the quickness with which the Egyptians report Sarai's beauty to Pharaoh and take her to his palace.

Rather than trusting his family to God's protecting hand, as he had just done in traveling from Haran to Canaan, Abram fashions a falsehood. He instructs Sarai (12:11–13) to say that she is his sister and to disguise the fact that she is his wife. This lie leads to a crisis. Pharaoh and his household are afflicted with serious diseases. God directly intervenes (12:17–20) so that Sarai might be spared and the lifeline that will lead to the world's Savior can continue. Pharaoh restores Sarai to Abram and sends Abram away.

Do you see God's unfathomable grace here? Even when Abram's sin threatens disaster, God sets things right! God's grace is greater than Abram's doubt! God's sure promise will carry Abram's family through its failures!

Don't we experience this same mix of faith and fear? Doesn't our faith shine brightly at one moment, only to flicker in the winds of doubt the next? But, as with Abram, God's grace reaches out to us. God keeps His promise to us. In Abram's line comes that display of God's love that would redeem our language and our lives. In Christ, our faith is secure. We are (Romans 4:11), by faith, the children of Abram. In Abram's Seed the confusion of Babel is replaced by a clearly stated promise (12:3): "All peoples on earth will be blessed through you."

Conclusion

Pentecost pictures the consequences of such a blessing. Earth's many languages unite in praise and adoration of Abram's saving Seed. Not prideful rebellion, but grateful praise is the language that Abram's Seed—the world's Messiah—has brought into our lives. In Him, through whom alone all blessings come, we have reason to use our lips and language for the splendid purpose of reunion with God and with one another. In Christ, such unity is already ours!

Concluding Activities

Confess the Apostles' Creed and pray the Lord's Prayer together to express your common faith. *(You may need to duplicate copies of these if any in your group may not know these by heart. If you do so, give everyone a copy so as not to single out anyone.)* Encourage participants to read the articles "Genesis Points to Jesus" and "Walk before Me" in the enrichment magazine. Make any necessary announcements and distribute study leaflet 6.

Notes

The Lifeline Is Focused

Genesis 14–16

Preparing for the Session

Central Focus

This sixth lesson is a study in power and weakness, victory and defeat, as God reaffirms His promises to Abram, who continues to exhibit a great faith punctuated by occasional bouts of human doubt.

Objectives

That the participant, as a child of God and with the Holy Spirit's help, will be led to

1. acknowledge God's hand in the victories of His people;

2. recognize the need to avoid human alliances that might lead God's people away from Him;

3. learn how to trust God for the impossible.

Note for small-group leaders: Lesson notes and other materials you will need begin on page 80.

For the Lecture Leader

Once again the time frame for the session probably best fits a 10-minute devotion period and a 15-minute lecture presentation.

Session Plan

Worship

Begin the session with the hymn, devotion, and prayer. The words of the hymn and prayer are printed in the study leaflet. Note that accompaniment for the hymn can be found on the music CD that accompanies this course. If you plan to use it, find it on the disk and cue it up before class.

Devotion

Read Genesis 14:18–20: "Then Melchizedek king of Salem brought out bread and wine. He was priest of God Most High, and he blessed Abram, saying, "Blessed be Abram by God Most High, Creator of heaven and earth. And blessed be God Most High, who delivered your enemies into your hand."

In ancient Greece, when a ship needed to enter a harbor, a small boat was sent in first to determine the positions of dangerous rocks, sandbars, and currents that might be destructive to a larger vessel. The small boat was called the *prodromos,* which means "guide" or "forerunner." The Book of Hebrews uses the same word to describe Jesus our High Priest: "We have this hope as an anchor for the soul, firm and secure. It enters the inner sanctuary behind the curtain, where Jesus, who went before us, has entered on our behalf. He has become a high priest forever, in the order of Melchizedek" (Hebrews 6:19–20).

Scott Walker tells of an American reconnaissance team sent out to scout enemy lines during World War II. On one mission they first had to cross an American minefield to reach German territory. No problem. They had a map identifying the warning markers. But just as they got across, they were pinned down by German machine-gun fire. The platoon was stopped in its tracks for hours, knowing that the German army would be advancing soon. A temporary retreat back across the minefield was the only answer. However, freshly fallen snow had covered all markers!

The quick-thinking American lieutenant ordered, "I'll go first. You follow 30 yards apart. Walk in my footsteps. That way, if I hit a mine, I alone will be killed." Walking precisely in the tracks of their leader, the platoon made it to safety. As they looked back over the field, it seemed as if only one person with one set of tracks had crossed the minefield.

Like that small boat or that lieutenant, Jesus is our forerunner, the one who has gone before us, just as

Melchizedek is considered a forerunner of the Christ, due to the type of priestly office he held. Each year a high priest from the line of Aaron would go before the people and enter the Most Holy Place to make atonement for them. But Jesus' priesthood is different, as different as Melchizedek's was from Aaron's.

The Levitical priesthood was hereditary and temporary, but the priestly order of Melchizedek is eternal and not based on heredity. Furthermore, Jesus, like Melchizedek, was something that no priest of Aaron could be—a king. Jesus is even more. He is our Prophet, Priest, and King, who has gone before us to secure a place in heaven for anyone who calls on His name.

Lecture Presentation

This lecture also appears on the CD-ROM that accompanies this course. Also look at the PDFFILES directory on the CD-ROM for visual aids available for the course.

Introduction

How do you picture the patriarchs? What did they look like? What sort of life did they live?

Genesis 14, 15, and 16 open a window on the world of the patriarchs. They hold before us a snapshot of Abram and his family. In fact, their description of Abram is much more like a movie than a snapshot—the action of armies clashing; the arrival of a strange priest; the appearance of God in the night. These exciting events provide insights into the patriarchal lifestyle.

1 A Day in the Life of Abram (14:1–17)

Abram's days were far from tranquil and quiet! Here we see the action-packed life of one who lives in the middle of real dangers. Genesis 14 places us in the center of an armed conflict. The events sweep Abram into combat! Verses 1–2 portray the contest between one military alliance and another. The forces of each side are described in detail:

> Amraphel, king of Shinar; Arioch, king of Ellasar; Kedorlaomer, king of Elam; and Tidal, king of Goiim;

Versus:

> Bera, king of Sodom; Birsha, king of Gomorrah; Shinab, king of Admah; Shemeber, king of Zeboiim; and Zoar, king of Bela.

Display visual 6A from the CD-ROM here. If the CD-ROM is not available, you may make a simple diagram on a chalkboard, listing the names of the kings on one side in one column, the names of the other kings in an opposing column, with opposing arrows between. Write the names of Abram and Lot also between the opposing columns of names to show that they were caught in the middle of this war.

This struggle reflects the political and cultural world in which Abram moved. Politically, Palestine was divided into small circles of influence. A fortified city lay at the center of each such circle and served as the seat of power. The ruler or king of each region had absolute power and ruled as he thought best.

Some of these kings ruled well! An inscription unearthed in this region celebrates the virtue of King Eirukagina "for firing dishonest tax collectors and other tainted officials, for giving amnesty to citizens unjustly imprisoned, and for decrees which protected the common citizen." The inscription dates from around 2350 B.C., the same era in which Abram lived.

But other kings used their power and privileged position to exploit the common folk. Their greed is revealed as archaeology uncovers the contrast between their lavish palaces and the paltry dwellings of their subjects.

This division of Palestine into small city-states, not unlike those of medieval Europe, frequently resulted in conflict. Access to water, land for grazing, trade routes, and countless other commodities was often contested.

Abram's world, so remote from us in time and place, is very close when we think about the tensions that come as people today try to live together. When our country is attacked or declares war, our families are immediately involved! Sons and daughters board planes or ships for remote regions of the world. Children cry themselves to sleep because they miss Daddy or Mommy. Community life is disrupted.

This is precisely what happened to Abram! Two alliances of city-states battled. Lot, Abram's nephew, was carried off by the forces that swept across Sodom (14:12). When a survivor of the battle reports Lot's capture, Abram springs into action. He summons the combat-ready men of his household for a rescue operation. Abram is joined by 318 men. This number gives us an approximate measure of Abram's wealth. His sheep, cattle, donkeys, and camels were attended by several hundred men. Their families as well would have lived under Abram's guidance and protection.

That Abram was familiar with armed conflict is indicated by the strategy he employs in Lot's rescue. He (14:15) divides his forces and attacks at night.

Display visual 6B from the CD-ROM here.

Genesis 14 indicates, however, that Abram regards his victory as a gift of God rather than the product of his military genius. It is crucial to note this dimension of Abram's character. He gives the credit to the God whom he confesses. This becomes clear in his response to the king of Sodom, who wanted Abram to keep the booty of the battle. Abram replies (14:22–23): "I have raised my hand to the LORD, God Most High, Creator of heaven and earth, and have taken an oath that I will accept nothing belonging to you, not even a thread or the thong of a sandal, so that you will never be able to say, 'I made Abram rich.' "

Abram's emphatic response is significant. The words "not even a thread or the thong of a sandal" alert us to the importance of this issue for the patriarch. Abram will not compromise his position! The holiness of the Lord, God Most High, must be upheld! Sodom's sinfulness has no place among God's people. Any hint that the values of Sodom can be associated with the Lord, God Most High, is to be removed.

Moreover, Abram's faith and character are revealed in his meeting with the priest of God Most High. We turn to this meeting now.

2 A Remarkable Priest: Melchizedek (14:18–24)

Display visual 6C from the CD-ROM here.

As Abram returns from defeating Kedorlaomer, he is met (14:17–18) by Melchizedek, king of Salem. This remarkable figure stands out for several reasons. First, though the Levitical priesthood was not yet instituted, Melchizedek (literally, "king of righteousness") was a priest of God as well as king of Salem (a shorter term for Jerusalem—Psalm 76:2). Second, his sudden appearance, without introduction or genealogy, points ahead to Christ, the great High Priest and the Prince of Peace to come (Hebrews 7).

The purpose of Melchizedek's appearance is also pivotal (14:19–20): "He blessed Abram, saying, 'Blessed be Abram by God Most High. ... And blessed be God Most High, who delivered your enemies into your hand.' " Again the blessing of God makes all the difference in Genesis! Far more than polite or pious sentiment, such a blessing brings into being the good things it invokes. The blessing of God Most High means those very things will happen! God Most High guarantees it!

The implications of chapter 14 for our life of faith are clear. Perhaps our crises more frequently have to do with money, work, or relationship issues, but as children of God who are also wandering through a foreign land, we know the challenges will come. With Abram we can commit every crisis to the gracious God who has blessed us. We trust the blessing that our great High Priest, Jesus Christ, has bestowed in His death for us. That blessing covers every sin and soothes every sadness. It brings deliverance and delight. It will not be revoked. Our Baptism has buried us in the blessing of our great High Priest.

3 God's Gracious Covenant: Its Promises Are Good (15:1–6)

Once again in Genesis 15 God appears to Abram. As in 12:7, God comes to assure Abram of His presence (15:1). God knew this assurance was needed. Abram's concern over his lack of an heir reaches a climax in the cry (15:2): "O Sovereign LORD, what can You give me since I remain childless and the one who will inherit my estate is Eliezer of Damascus?" This cry reflects the ancient law that permitted a servant to become the legal heir in the case of a childless master.

God counters (15:4) that this will most certainly not be

the case! To give definite and visible form to this promise, God leads Abram out into the desert night. He invites Abram to look at the stars of the heaven, to count their great numbers. Abram's offspring will outnumber even the stars. Astronomers suggest that at least 8,000 stars would have been visible to Abram's naked eye. With today's sophisticated telescopes we can see billions more! What an illustration and consolation!

At the age of 75 plus, it would have been easy for Abram to doubt or even despair. The years had passed. God had repeated His promises. Yet, still there was no son!

Genesis 15:6 leaps at us from the pages of sacred Scripture: "Abram believed the LORD, and He credited it to him as righteousness." In the face of his frustration and anxiety, Abram "believed the LORD." This trust in God's promise is "credited to him as righteousness." It is striking that there is no hint here of moral heroism. Scripture has shared with us Abram's sins. His weakness is clearly evident. But, in the midst of frailty, his faith rests on the promise of God!

By grace we stand beside Abram. Our faith shines not from the polished pedestal of a perfect life. Rather, in the same arena of daily anxiety our faith rests on the grace of God shown to us in our Savior and His cross.

As we consider Abram's faith we must remember its context—the Lord's gracious promise! God would give Abram a son. Even more significantly, this son would be the father of the messianic line (Galatians 3:6–9). The lifeline continues! The promised Messiah, the Offspring of the woman, the Seed of Seth, Noah, Shem, and now Abram—God's promised Messiah—would crush the serpent's head. This Seed would replace the curse of the fall with a blessing upon all believers.

4 An Appearance in the Night (15:7–21)

The rest of Genesis 15 describes a graphic reminder God gave Abram to reinforce the truth of His faithfulness. First (15:7) God identifies Himself as the one "who brought you out of Ur of the Chaldeans to give you this land." Then He affirms His promise with an oath.

While the sacrifice of a heifer, a goat, and a ram may seem strange to our ears, we would be wrong to view

this as a primitive or superstitious ritual. The God who created the world and called it good uses elements from that world to instruct Abram. What we see is a smoking firepot with a blazing torch passing between the pieces of the sacrificed animals. This gracious use of earthly elements demonstrates God's presence. This ritual ratifies and reinforces (vv. 13–16) the promises of God and consecrates (v. 18) the covenant relationship.

5 The Human Side of a Divine Promise (16:1–16)

Chapter 16 comforts each generation of the faithful with the Good News that God's promise is trustworthy. God's promise penetrates the barriers of inept or evil human actions.

Seeking to be helpful, Sarai further complicates Abram's situation. Ancient laws from this period permitted a childless woman to present her maid to her husband. The child of the maid would be viewed legally as the child of her mistress. Sarai, aware of this practice and frustrated by the fact she has not conceived a son (16:2), presents Abram with her maidservant Hagar. But, as we may have experienced ourselves, human intervention to aid or accelerate God's plan can bring delay and disappointment. What Sarai thought would bring long-awaited fulfillment quickly became a miserable failure. Hagar, in an all-too-human manner (16:4), "began to despise her mistress." Sarai, reflecting her disappointment, blames Abram for this development (16:5): "You are responsible for the wrong I am suffering."

Still, rather than inviting us to focus on the failures of Abram and Sarai, chapter 16 holds before us God's faithfulness. Despite the rancor that resulted, despite the strife, the Lord does not abandon Abram! The Lord's blessing covers all in Abram's house. The angel of the Lord (16:7) will even go to a desert place for the sake of a servant girl! The instruction to return to Abram's house is joined to a great promise (16:10): "I will so increase your descendants that they will be too numerous to count." Hagar too receives the Lord's gracious promise!

Conclusion

The gritty grace of God shines through this sin-engendered strife. God does not give up even when we mess up everything! Genesis 14–16 display the character of Abram's God. And when our own lives are marked by the same sort of mess—domestic strife, fearful flight, bitter fights—we can turn to a God who is always there for us.

That lifeline from Abram to Christ is focused and firm. It is for us! The Lord (12:3) guarantees the birth of Abram's seed in whom all earth's nations will be blessed. Whatever unfolds from history's pages, this lifeline will continue. It cannot be cut. The promise is certain. Those who trust in the Messiah today, in spite of all that happens along life's way, are truly the children of Abram (Galatians 3:7)!

Concluding Activities

Close with a brief period of silent reflection in which all are asked to review how they have looked to God for His leading and have trusted Him during this past week. Follow the silence by speaking a brief prayer, asking God's forgiveness for lack of trust in Him and for the Holy Spirit's help in developing a greater trust in God. Then perhaps speak a blessing or benediction. Encourage participants to read the articles "Covenants in Genesis" and "God's Family Plan" in the enrichment magazine. Make necessary announcements and distribute study leaflet 7.

Notes

The Lifeline in Abraham

Genesis 17–19

Preparing for the Session

Central Focus

These three chapters reiterate a continuing theme in Genesis: judgment and grace. Judgment is demonstrated in the destruction of wicked Sodom and Gomorrah, but grace is in God's gift of the covenant sign of circumcision and in His deliverance of Lot and his daughters from destruction.

Objectives

That the participant, as a child of God and with the Holy Spirit's help, will be led to

1. treasure Baptism as God's covenant of grace;
2. better understand the power and process of intercessory prayer and grow in commitment to such prayer;
3. understand and rely on God's grace in the midst of His judgment.

Note for small-group leaders: Lesson notes and other materials you will need begin on page 83.

For the Lecture Leader

Continue in this and the last two sessions with any needed adjustments in the time schedule for large-group worship, small-group discussion, and the lecture presentation.

Session Plan

Worship

Begin the session with the hymn, devotion, and prayer. The words of the hymn and prayer are printed in the study leaflet. Note that accompaniment for the hymn can be found on the music CD that accompanies this course. If you plan to use it, find it on the disk and cue it up before class.

Devotion

Read Genesis 18:32–33: "Then [Abraham] said, 'May the Lord not be angry, but let me speak just once more. What if only ten can be found there?' [The Lord] answered, 'For the sake of ten, I will not destroy it.' When the Lord had finished speaking with Abraham, He left, and Abraham returned home."

Alfred, Lord Tennyson once wrote, "More things are wrought by prayer than this world dreams of." And then he went on to accuse men of being no better than mindless sheep or goats "if, knowing God, they lift not hands of prayer both for themselves and those who call them friends."

Jesus prayed for His friends. So did St. Paul. And so did Abraham, as we see in this week's LifeLight lesson. In fact, he even interceded for a town full of sexually immoral men! Nor did he have any qualms about his prayer posture, as he bowed down and begged, cajoled, and negotiated with the Lord in the process. Proper prayer etiquette has never been a priority for any of God's children who believe in the power of prayer.

And God listened to Abraham's prayer. He was willing to spare the wicked cities of Sodom and Gomorrah for the sake of just 10 righteous people. But even that turned out to be too high a standard, and God destroyed the cities by raining down burning sulfur.

In spite of that, Abraham's persistence in prayer is an example for us to follow. A famous California car dealer claims he "will stand upon his head until his face is turning red" in order to sell an auto. Are you that persistent in your prayer life? Are you as persistent as Abraham?

Martin Luther remarked that Scripture "teaches us the real art of begging, teaches us to be positively obtrusive, unabashed, and endlessly persistent before God. For he who is timid soon permits himself to be turned away and is not fit for begging. We must shed all shyness and consider that our Lord God wants to have us urge and persevere. For to give much is His delight and glory, and He is pleased if we expect much good from Him."[1]

Intercessory prayer takes persistence, sometimes because the souls for whom we are praying don't even want to be prayed for! But don't let a little thing like that stop you. It certainly didn't stop Abraham.

[1]Ewald M. Plass, comp. *What Luther Says: An Anthology*, Volume 2 (St. Louis: Concordia, 1959), 1089.

Lecture Presentation

This lecture also appears on the CD-ROM that accompanies this course. Also look at the PDFFILES directory on the CD-ROM for visual aids available for the course.

Introduction

What is your idea of the ideal lifestyle? To young couples with growing families and incomes that never seem to stretch far enough, the ideal lifestyle might seem to include lots of money and few responsibilities. Frustrations may even lead some married persons to yearn for the freedom of being single.

On the other hand, single individuals may long for marriage and children. And the hearts of childless couples may ache for children.

1 Patriarchal Priorities (Genesis 17)

Abram, along with the whole biblical world of his day, regarded children as a great blessing. If some adults today regard children as a burden, Abram's generation viewed them as an essential ingredient in the good life (Psalm 128:3–6). So central was this conviction to Abram and Sarah that their childlessness created a crisis. God had promised them a son, an heir, repeatedly. Yet year after year passed while they remained childless.

Display visual 7A from the CD-ROM here.

Chapter 17 opens with a statement about Abram's age (v. 1): "When Abram was ninety-nine years old." This focus on Abram's age sets the stage for another appearance by God Almighty. God appears in order to repeat His divine promise in a dramatic way. God is going to change the name Abram ("exalted father") to Abraham ("father of many"). This name change (v. 5) will reflect God's work in Abraham—"for I have made you a father of many nations."

We should not miss the irony of Abraham's position! On one hand were God's repeated promises of offspring. These promises were richly illustrated. God invited Abram to count the stars in the heavens, this as a hint of the vast numbers of his descendants. Now, his very name would be changed to underscore this promise. Still, on the other hand, Abraham grows old. But he does not have even one single child by Sarah! The contrast between God's promises and Abram's reality becomes more and more noticeable.

We can say the same for Sarai. God changes her name from Sarai ("princess") to Sarah ("princess and mother"). God will make Sarah (17:16) the "mother of nations; kings of peoples will come from her."

This increasing contradiction between God's claims and Abraham's current condition finally overwhelms him (17:17): "Abraham fell facedown; he laughed and said to himself, 'Will a son be born to a man a hundred years old? Will Sarah bear a child at the age of ninety?' "

Display visual 7B from the CD-ROM here.

Doesn't Abraham mirror our temperament? Aren't we sometimes impatient with God's timing? Doesn't there sometimes appear to be a contradiction between God's promise and our experience? Like a child who begins to wonder whether Christmas will ever come, we can grow weary of waiting. We can cry out like Abraham. We can even complain.

Abraham phrases his cry in language that gives God an easy way out (17:18): "If only Ishmael might live under Your blessing!" God immediately clarifies the claim for Abraham (17:19): "Yes, but your wife Sarah will bear you a son, and you will call him Isaac. I will establish

My covenant with him." God promises (17:20) to bless Ishmael, nevertheless His covenant will be established with Isaac (17:21), "whom Sarah will bear to you by this time next year." This repetition rivets the promise to Abraham and Sarah. God's promise is clear; the parentage of the promised son is certain.

Abraham's laughter at the implausibility of the promise will be echoed in its fulfillment. A son born to Sarah and Abraham—not Ishmael—will be named Isaac, that is, "he laughs."

The fact that Abraham's faith embraces this promise, despite all contrary evidence, is proven by his obedience. He (17:23–27) circumcises his whole household. God stipulated (17:11) that circumcision would serve as a distinctive sign of His covenant promise to Abram: "You are to undergo circumcision, and it will be the sign of the covenant between Me and you." God knows we are physical creatures, formed from the dust of the earth. Thus, He uses physical means, and visible means, to establish His covenant word to Abraham—and to us! Water. Bread. Wine.

So central is circumcision to God's covenant that (17:13) any foreigners or slaves who live in Abraham's household are to undergo this rite. Anyone not circumcised is to be (17:14) "cut off from his people," excluded from the chosen nation Abraham will become.

The theological parallel with Baptism is clear. The Sacraments are statements, not of God's judgment on sin, but of His gracious promise of a saving seed. Isaac will continue that "lifeline" that would reverse the curse of sin. The Savior, the Offspring of the woman we first read about in Genesis 3:15, will come from Abraham through Isaac. This truth makes circumcision as well as Baptism more than a mere option. Both circumcision and Baptism incorporate us into Christ. Both rites are central to God's kingdom. His Old Testament people saw the Gospel significance in circumcision; His New Testament people see that significance in Baptism.

Abraham saw it. And so (17:27), at the age of 99, Abraham is circumcised, together with Ishmael and Abraham's entire household.

2 Yet Another Announcement (Genesis 18:1–19)

God's grace shines forth in manifold actions. Chapter 18 describes another appearance of the Lord God to Abraham.

The setting is almost too simple. As is still the case in nomadic cultures, Abraham sought shelter from the midday sun by sitting (18:1) "at the entrance to his tent." Suddenly he sees three men standing nearby. The strong stress on hospitality that marked the ancient world is reflected in (18:3–8) his hurried preparation of a lavish meal. Modern visitors to the Middle East experience the same sort of warmth. Only the best is to be provided for the guest!

As the three men eat, they inquire about Sarah (18:9). One of the men, identified now as "the LORD," announces that by the time of His return next year Sarah will have a son. Sarah had been listening near the entrance of the tent. What could these three men want with her husband? What was their aim? When Sarah overhears the announcement of her pregnancy, she can't help but giggle. Aware of her age, Sarah's laugh of disbelief (18:12) echoes that of Abraham's a bit earlier. The Lord calls attention to Sarah's response (18:13) not to make her a spectacle, but to affirm that what was promised will come to pass.

The drama of these events can hardly be overstressed. In a culture that delighted in children, the great patriarch and his wife remained barren! They had everything, but, at the same time, they had nothing.

Except for God's promises. Promises. It seemed this was all they had. Though they believed in and served God, the years rolled on until, humanly speaking, hope was gone.

Display visual 7C from the CD-ROM here.

Doesn't our faith waver in similar fashion? We believe God, but how easily we drift into doubt and even despair over whether His promises will come to pass.

Abraham and Sarah could be assaulted by doubts from *within* just as we are. But they were also faced with challenges from *without*! As Abraham walks with his three visitors, the Lord repeats His gracious promise (18:18) that all the nations on earth will be blessed through his offspring. An important aspect of this renewed promise is its accent on what is to follow (18:19): "For I have chosen him, so that he will direct his children and his household after him to keep the way of the LORD by doing what is right and just, so that the LORD will bring about for Abraham what He has promised him."

God's gracious promise invites a life that reflects His presence and power. The family or community or nation called together by this promise appropriately (18:19) "keep[s] the way of the LORD by doing what is right and just." God's promise is not suspended in the heavens. His covenant is not up in the clouds somewhere. God will give Abraham a son who will father a great nation. Isaac and the nation of Israel are to keep the way of the Lord. Abraham and all his children are to live in the light of this glorious promise. Abraham (Hebrews 11:10) "was looking forward to the city with foundations, whose architect and builder is God."

3 The Sinful City (Genesis 18:20–19:38)

Seth stood out in his generation; Noah in his. Now Abraham stands out in sharp contrast to those around him. Sodom and its sister city, Gomorrah, were not far from Abraham's flocks. But the city Abraham looked for and these two cities were literally worlds apart. They could not coexist.

Not the way of the Lord, but the way of great and grievous sin was the path to Sodom and Gomorrah (18:20). All the appearances of prosperity that so appealed to Lot were artificial. The substance of these cities was sinful rebellion against the Lord's will for His creatures. As with sections of Hollywood, Las Vegas, and the nightspots of today's major and not-so-major cities, the lights and glitter frequently disguised the darkness of the deeds done there.

How striking that sacred Scripture devotes a long section to the dialogue between God and Abraham near Sodom and Gomorrah (18:16–33). We puzzle over Abraham's persistence in pleading for these sorry cities. What motivated him? Why this lengthy exchange? To both questions, the answer is God's grace. Abraham knew the gracious character of God. He knew the Lord

is disposed to bring redemption, not ruin, to nations. He himself had experienced this "gritty grace" as the Lord had stayed with him in spite of his own sin. So Abraham, as God's chosen prophet (20:7) appeals to God's gracious character.

This explains his persistence in petitioning the Lord over and over. Time after time, as Abraham negotiates a lower threshold of righteousness, the Lord replies: For the sake of _____, I will not destroy it (18:26–31). **You may, on a chalkboard, write—and successively cross out—the numbers 50, 45, 40, 20, and 10—but do not cross out the 10.** Finally, the Lord grants that even for the sake of 10 He will not destroy the city. Despite the wickedness that cries out to heaven, the Lord will relent for the sake of only 10 who walk in His way! No mathematical distribution of justice is displayed here. Sodom and Gomorrah deserved destruction. But God's grace, so great in its influence, would override every formula. For the sake of only a handful, the whole population would be spared!

Display visual 7D from the CD-ROM here.

Such a God does not give up! Through Abraham's son, through the lifeline we have repeatedly studied in Genesis, God would send His own Son so that the whole of humanity might be saved for the sake of one. **Write a 1 on the chalkboard. Underline it.** In Christ we are the beneficiaries of this grace. Abraham had experienced it. His one Seed would bless all the nations! In Christ, the fate of all was reduced to the presence of that one. And, in Christ, the Holy One enters human history! For His sake, and for His sake alone, God has pronounced a blessing upon all the inhabitants of the earth. His grace has extended itself to the cross where Abraham's Son— God's own dearly beloved Son—offers up His life.

The tragedy of prideful rejection unfolds in chapter 19. God's grace is dismissed. The sorry story of Genesis 3 is repeated. People select sin and reject salvation. The scene in Sodom remains as seedy as any X-rated movie. The angels, in human form, are welcomed by Lot. But they are also sought out by the men of Sodom. Ancient cities were very sensitive to the presence of strangers. Their coming was quickly noted for they could be spies. The men of Sodom, however, sought the visitors out, and not for reasons of security. They were searching for some new and sordid sexual pleasure (19:5–10).

Finally, the affront to God's messengers had to be met. The searching eyes of Sodom (19:11) are struck blind. Perpetual darkness soon envelops the whole population as (19:24–25, 28) the cities are utterly destroyed. The contrast between God's grace upon those who receive it and His judgment upon those who spurn it is very stark (19:29): "So when God destroyed the cities of the plain, He remembered Abraham, and He brought Lot out of the catastrophe that overthrew the cites where Lot had lived."

The same contrast still exists. Those who reject grace will bear the consequences of sin! Those who are by grace in Christ are delivered!

Concluding Activities

Close the assembly with an intercessory prayer. Ask for names of persons or groups of people to be included. (You may want to make some suggestions of your own.) Be ready with pencil and paper to list those who are suggested. Then offer the prayer. Encourage participants to read "Veiled in Shame" in the enrichment magazine. Make necessary announcements and distribute study leaflet 8.

Notes

The Lifeline through Isaac

Genesis 20–22

Preparing for the Session

Central Focus

Considering Abraham's dealings with Abimelech and Hagar, "history repeats itself" might be an appropriate theme for this study. However, Abraham's testing, central to the covenant lifeline theme of Genesis, dominates this lesson.

Objectives

That the participant, as a child of God and with the Holy Spirit's help, will be led to

1. learn from mistakes rather than repeat them;

2. recognize God's grace and provision, active even toward those whom others have rejected;

3. trust God more completely in times of testing;

4. thank God for the sacrifice of His Son.

Note for small-group leaders: Lesson notes and other materials you will need begin on page 86.

For the Lecture Leader

The first two chapters of this lesson tend to be overshadowed by Genesis 22, and for good reason. Despite all of Abraham's weaknesses in the past, his test in chapter 22 confirms that the faith credited to him as righteousness was genuine after all.

Be sensitive to the tension God purposely puts on Abraham's lifeline by ordering the sacrifice of his son and heir, Isaac. Do not neglect to mention Abraham's hope and belief in the resurrection, attested to in Genesis 22:5 and Hebrews 11:17–19, for this hope remains our central hope also in times of testing.

Session Plan

Worship

Begin the session with the hymn, devotion, and prayer. The words of the hymn are printed in the study leaflet. Note that accompaniment for the hymn can be found on the music CD that accompanies this course. If you plan to use it, find it on the disk and cue it up before class.

Devotion

On May 29, 1953, at 11:30 A.M., Sir Edmund Hillary became famous by planting a British flag atop Mount Everest. He was the first man to achieve that monumental feat, climaxing long, strenuous months of planning and training. Hillary had to become acclimated to the height and cold weather. He had to stockpile supplies. Heavily burdened by equipment, he and his crew crawled their way upward, knowing that death waited for them in every crevice. But eventually he and his partner stood over 29,000 feet above sea level. No one had ever made a more difficult climb.

But is that really the case?

By the time Abraham and Isaac had reached the peak of Mount Moriah, they had made a far more difficult climb. Mount Moriah—very near another small mount that one day would be called Calvary—represented the highest possible pinnacle of surrender. For it was there that Abraham surrendered his Isaac. Few men have ever climbed as high or been as willing to sacrifice as much—except the heavenly Father, who also surrendered His "Isaac," His only-begotten Son, in the greatest sacrifice ever offered.

You and I have many "Isaacs" in our lives—people and things extremely precious to us. We would find it difficult to give them up. But what could be more precious to us than the free gift of eternal life itself? What sacrifice of thanksgiving on our part could ever say thank You enough in thankfulness to Christ who climbed Calvary's hill for us?

When Christ beckons us to surrender one of our precious "Isaacs" and to take up His cross and follow Him, surrender is no disgrace. It is a climb well made and a sacrifice well worth it.

Lecture Presentation

This lecture also appears on the CD-ROM that accompanies this course. Also look at the PDFFILES directory on the CD-ROM for visual aids available for the course.

Introduction

How frequently do you travel? When was your last family vacation? Most of us enjoy "getting away" once in awhile, even if we don't go far or stay long. **You might mention a recent vacation trip of your own. It's fun to have a change of pace and see a new place!**

Traveling can also be frightening! A flat tire. A faulty fuel pump. What would be easy to fix at home can be life threatening on a trip! Who will stop to help us? Can they be trusted not to harm us? **Do you recall a personal experience you might mention?**

Such sentiments are not new. They have always been a part of travel. If anything, ancient travel was even more dangerous. Banditry was frequent. Hostile princes could pounce on anyone moving through their realm.

Yet, as patriarch of a nomadic family, Abraham had to travel. It was part of his job. He supported his large family by means of the flocks and herds in his care. Food, clothing, and shelter were all tied to these animals. Without adequate water and good grazing, Abraham's family would be threatened with extinction. The line of life would be cut off!

1 A Failure of Faith (Genesis 20)

Genesis 20 begins with Abraham's movement: "Now Abraham moved on from there into the region of the Negev" (20:1).

Movement. Travel. It was the mark of the nomadic lifestyle. The mobility of many in our modern culture provides a rough parallel. An employee on the way up from the assembly line to the executive office may well be transferred from plant to plant.

Genesis 20 shows Abraham going south into the region of the Negev. As he travels, the safety and security of known surroundings are left behind, and fear of the unknown surfaces. Abraham pauses as he enters the lands of Abimelech. His fear was not without foundation. Regional kings habitually exploited travelers. Flocks, herds, and prospective slaves presented a tempting target, representing enormous wealth and income. Whole families simply disappeared as they crossed into unknown regions!

These were the facts of life Abraham faced. These facts explain what seems very strange to us. Again, Abraham represents Sarah as his sister! Abraham's fear of Abimelech, like his fear of Pharaoh, leads to a failure of faith and behavior. Abraham fails to tell the truth and creates another crisis.

This time the circumstances are a bit different. In chapter 12 Sarai's beauty attracts the Egyptians' attention. But in chapter 20 Abimelech appears to be following common diplomatic protocol. In the ancient Near East treaties were customarily sealed by a marriage. The head of one nation would marry a prominent member of the other prince's or patriarch's clan. This marriage, it was thought, would minimize the possibility of war and maximize the strength of the bond. This practice also partially explains the growth of large harems. A prince who had allied himself with several neighbors would multiply the number of his wives through these treaties.

This background sheds light on the simple description (20:1–2): "For a while he stayed in Gerar, and there Abraham said of his wife Sarah, 'She is my sister.' Then Abimelech king of Gerar sent for Sarah and took her."

Again Abraham's sinful nature leads him into a real mess. To confess his lie and retrieve Sarah would create an even greater crisis for all concerned.

Doesn't this sound all too familiar? Haven't we seen our faith and trust in God flicker and cause crises and complications—perhaps worse consequences than the ones we were trying to avoid in the first place?

But again, God, in grace, intervenes to deliver Abraham's line! The Lord appears to Abimelech in a dream, warning him that Sarah is Abraham's wife. God's intervention brings a blessing to all! Abimelech (20:17–18) and his whole household are healed. Abraham (20:14–16) receives permission to live in the land, and he receives many gifts from Abimelech.

2 At Long Last—The Promised Seed (Genesis 21:1–7)

For a child, waiting can be painful. Can you recall when, as a child, you waited for Christmas? Will it ever get here? That's the question even adults ask while waiting for something special.

Chapter 21 opens with the beautiful, almost understated, assertion that God's promise has come to pass. So long awaited, the promise comes to pass precisely as God had said. This complete consistency between God's word and God's deed cannot be missed. The promise that had seemed like empty words for so long now becomes a new and wonderful reality. What God said He would do, He now does (21:1): "Now the LORD was gracious to Sarah as He had said, and the LORD did for Sarah what He had promised."

Abraham and Sarah (12:1–3) had waited 25 years since God had made that promise. The Bible doesn't play down their inner turmoil as they waited for the fulfillment of that promise (15:1–3; 17:17; 18:12). Over and over the Lord repeated His promise despite the failing hopes and nagging doubts of Abraham and Sarah.

Display visual 8A from the CD-ROM here.

And now the empty nest is filled. It is filled with laughter! From Abraham's naming of Isaac (v. 3) to Sarah's reflection (v. 6), there is laughter all around! "Sarah said, 'God has brought me laughter, and everyone who hears about this will laugh with me.' " Abraham's line will go on! The lifeline that ran from Seth through Shem to Abraham, the line that would lead to the woman's Offspring, the woman's Seed, the Messiah, is now alive and well in the birth of Isaac. The whole human family can laugh in joy.

Life, the full and abundant life, was present even then. The laughter of Abraham and Sarah is contagious! As Christians we laugh along, for we see in this birth the future birth that would bring a blessing to the whole of creation. In Isaac's birth Jesus' birth is foreshadowed.

Display visual 8B from the CD-ROM here.

Reflect for a moment. If your life seems ho-hum and humdrum, if it sometimes seems to have more disappointment and doubts than heavenly happenings, take heart. You're in good company! You're in the company of the faithful saints (Hebrews 11). Like Abraham and Sarah, your waiting will be rewarded! God's deeds will match His words! You can laugh! Even more closely than Abraham and Sarah, you have beheld the birth that penetrates the whole earth's uneasiness. Your sin has met its match. The birth of God's Son has delivered each of us from our own line of death as Adam's children. For in Christ we also are Abraham's children, grafted into his lifeline. In Isaac that line was continued so that we might be saved.

Still, until the return of Christ, we mingle our laughter with longing. All the promises of God have not been fulfilled. We long for that day of fullness still to come. So it was with Abraham. Isaac's birth brought laughter. God had kept His word. But, His word still came to a sinful human race. Abraham had not yet arrived in heaven.

3 Problems—Within and Without (Genesis 21:8–34)

Two events continued to cloud the full clarity of God's promises: the rivalry of Ishmael (21:8–21) and tension with Abimelech (21:22–34).

A. The Rivalry of Ishmael (Genesis 21:8–21)

Genesis doesn't disguise difficulty. It doesn't suggest all will be well for the child of God in all ways all the time. In this way it describes a world we readily recognize. Just when things appear to be perfect, a problem disturbs our paradise!

So it was for Abraham and Sarah! Isaac was born! Laughter rang out! But suddenly—and sadly—another sentiment surfaces: jealousy.

Jealousy. This age old enemy rears its ugly head. It punctures the peace. It mars the paradise. It provokes Abraham to action. The same jealousy that sneaks in and shatters our lives was at work in Abraham's family too.

In fact, jealousy splits the family (21:9–10). "But Sarah

saw that the son whom Hagar the Egyptian had borne to Abraham was mocking, and she said to Abraham, 'Get rid of that slave woman and her son.' " Abraham was caught. He loved his son Ishmael. He (v. 11) was reluctant. But God guides the lifeline.

Hagar and Ishmael were to leave with God's blessing. Both Abraham (v. 13) and Hagar (v. 18) were told that God would make Ishmael into a great nation. The tender and intimate attention (vv. 15–21) God gave to the needs of Hagar and Ishmael is touching. God's good hand (v. 19) provided a cup of water and (v. 20) attended Ishmael in his growing years.

B. Tension with Abimelech (Genesis 21:22–34)

Even as these tensions surfaced within the family, Abraham's encounter with Abimelech (vv. 25–26) posed problems from *without*. The potential for armed conflict is prominent. A dispute has surfaced over access to water—the one essential substance for life in the desert. Abimelech's men (v. 25) have seized a key well by force! From what we know of ancient cultures, few men would have engaged in such an action without the consent of their clan's chief. Probably Abimelech had ordered his men to seize the well. But whatever Abimelech's involvement, Abraham (v. 27) proposes a peace treaty.

This very well, the center of the dispute, has been uncovered by archaeologists at Beersheba. If this is not the *precise* well, it is one dating from the period and is located at the right place. The ring of reality attends these events even as we unearth the evidence of ancient excavators in search of water!

God's gracious hand blessed Abraham's efforts. Abraham recognized God's presence (v. 33): "Abraham planted a tamarisk tree in Beersheba, and there he called upon the name of the LORD, the Eternal God."

4 Abraham's Test (Genesis 22)

If God had settled matters within Abraham's family and protected him from challenges without, chapter 22 presents what appears impossible. Now the problem is God! God comes directly to Abraham and commands him to do the unthinkable! The text holds before us the horror of God's command to sacrifice Isaac.

This moving passage has inspired much speculation. Søren Kierkegaard, the Danish thinker, considered it the best biblical description of faith.

Try, for a moment, to enter Abraham's world. The long wait. The birth of Isaac. Despite Abraham's problems, Isaac provided continual pleasure to the patriarch. Abraham watched Isaac at play. He recalled his son's extraordinary birth. Abraham's whole life was invested in his long-awaited son.

But, now—could it be? Incredibly, God now comes and commands Abraham to sacrifice Isaac. God's words must have hit Abraham like hammer blows. The text seems to slow to a snail's pace as God repeats (22:2, emphasis added): "Take … your son, … your only son, … Isaac, … whom you love, … and go to the region of Moriah. … Sacrifice him there … as a burnt offering."

How could any father fathom such a command? Yet, Abraham rises early and organizes the journey. Verse 4 indicates that the journey took three days. Can you imagine how Abraham's thoughts must have tortured him along the way? Each word from Isaac must have rung in Abraham's ears. Every step would, as Abraham alone knew, bring them closer to the place … the place of sacrifice … the place of death. His son … so much alive and so great a joy … awaited for so long … would soon be silent! Reflect on how Isaac's own questions must have pierced the patriarch's heart (v. 7): "Father? … The fire and the wood are here … but where is the lamb for the burnt offering?"

"Where is the lamb?"

Abraham, as Hebrews 11:19 indicates, even now was full of trust. He trusted that God could raise Isaac. But this trust did not diminish the anguish Abraham faced. Why would God, who had given Isaac, request his death?

Genesis 22:1 reveals the reason for this incredible command: "God tested Abraham." What would such testing require? Quite simply God wanted Abraham to display his love. The key question: Would Abraham show more love for God or for Isaac?

We all know how it comes out. The angel of the Lord called out (22:12): "Do not lay a hand on the boy. … Do not do anything to him. Now I know that you fear

God, because you have not withheld from Me your son, your only son."

Display visual 8C from the CD-ROM here.

Not surprisingly, ancient Christians saw the divinely provided ram (22:13) as an image, or type, of Christ, the Lamb of God. Immediately after this grand deliverance (v. 17) comes a great blessing. In and through Isaac's line the divine blessing will come upon all! What a fitting close, for in this blessing the future of all of us is secure! God has provided the Lamb for us too!

Concluding Activities

Try this responsive prayer. End each of several parts of a prayer by saying, "For this evidence of Your love." The group responds by saying, "We thank You, Lord." Include among the parts of your prayer praise to God for giving His Son to be our Savior.

Encourage participants to read "Old Sins" in the enrichment magazine. Make necessary announcements and distribute study leaflet 9.

Notes

The Lifeline Expands

Genesis 23:1–25:11

Preparing for the Session

Central Focus

This final lesson in our study of the first half of Genesis encompasses the death of Sarah and Abraham but also the marriage of Isaac and Rebekah. The promise to Abraham will go on through his descendants.

Objectives

That the participant, as a child of God and with the Holy Spirit's help, will be led to

1. see this earth only as a temporary home for those who hold citizenship in heaven through their Baptism;

2. look to the guidance of God in the selection of a Christian mate;

3. praise God that His covenant promises do not die, even when people do.

Note for small-group leaders: Lesson notes and other materials you will need begin on page 89.

For the Lecture Leader

This study may begin and end with death, but sandwiched between the deaths of Sarah and Abraham is the assurance that the line of promise will continue through Isaac and Rebekah. Discussions about death and marriage may occupy major segments of the discussion time, but the theme of God preserving His messianic lifeline and His covenant promises should be the main thrust of the lesson.

The lecture leader will discover that the heart of the lecture centers on Genesis 24, the longest chapter in Genesis. How interesting that this longest chapter deals with marriage, the most important of all human relationships. The lecture describes how God's hand was crucial in bringing about this special bond between Isaac and Rebekah. The lecture leader must stress the theme of the Messiah's continuing lifeline since this is the final lecture of this course.

Session Plan

Worship

Begin the session with the hymn, devotion, and prayer. The words of the hymn are printed in the study leaflet. Note that accompaniment for the hymn can be found on the music CD that accompanies this course. If you plan to use it, find it on the disk and cue it up before class.

Devotion

Read Genesis 24:3–4: [Abraham said,] "I want you to swear by the LORD, the God of heaven and the God of earth, that you will not get a wife for my son from the daughters of the Canaanites, among whom I am living, but will go to my country and my own relatives and get a wife for my son Isaac."

Are you a tire kicker? a melon thumper? Do you refuse to buy the first commodity you're looking for until you investigate all the other places in town that sell the same item?

Some people can be extremely picky in their selections. It may even be rather aggravating to us as we watch their tedious trek to find the perfect choice—whether it be a new automobile on the showroom floor, a ripe watermelon at the grocery store, or the perfect mate with whom to share one's life.

When Abraham saw the need to find a wife for his son, he, too, was picky. He knew that to choose a pagan for Isaac would jeopardize the lifeline that was to lead to the Messiah. He also knew that not just any matchmaker could be entrusted to broker such an important transaction. He selected his trusted servant—a follower of the true God—to carry out his instructions to the letter. But most of all, Abraham and his servant both trusted in God, who—having guided them faithfully in the past—would certainly lead them to make the right choices.

For Christians today, too, the choice of a God-fearing mate is a priority. Indeed, we want to make all of our life choices in a God-pleasing way. This includes everything from major decisions, such as deciding on a career, to seemingly minor choices, such as what TV show to watch.

We worship the same God as did Abraham of old. He has guided our past decisions, and He is the one to whom we entrust our choices for the future. Things do not happen by mere chance. God has brought us safely and wisely to this time and place for a purpose. God-pleasing choices are necessarily picky choices, but the results will bring eternal dividends.

Lecture Presentation

This lecture also appears on the CD-ROM that accompanies this course. Also look at the PDFFILES directory on the CD-ROM for visual aids available for the course.

Introduction

Gail Sheehey has made a career studying and writing about "passages," points in time that separate all that will come after from all that has gone before. She thinks of passages as life stages. But the birth of a child, a marriage, a death of a spouse or parent—these moments also change things.

1 Death: The First Passage (Genesis 23)

Sarah's death was a passage for Abraham's family. The text of Genesis 23 draws our attention to its significance in several ways.

First, contrary to the usual practice, the Bible (23:1) records Sarah's age at her death. This underscores her key role in the messianic line. Her advanced age also suggests a full and complete life, a life God had brought to full fruition.

Her death reminds us of (chapter 3) the cause of

death—sin—and echoes (chapter 5) that litany of death repeated over each link in the family tree.

But—and here (23:3–4) the text turns our gaze to God's mercy—Abraham seeks to bury Sarah in the land of Canaan. The promise of the land was intimately tied to and intertwined with the promise of a family (Genesis 12:1–3). By dwelling on the fact that Sarah is to be buried in the land that God had promised, the text holds before us the certainty of the Gospel promise. God keeps His gracious Word!

Yet—and here we face an important characteristic of God's ways with Abraham and with us—God doesn't accomplish all of this with a loud voice and with lightning bolts from heaven. Abraham would bury Sarah in the Promised Land. But God wasn't going to intervene miraculously from above! Abraham would have to do some tough negotiating with an astute businessman (v. 10) named Ephron. The purchase of the cave of Machpelah displays a social and legal process requiring precise behavior by each party involved in the transaction. We see this in verses 3–20. Abraham conducted this business deal in a culture that expected he follow a strict protocol.

Display visual 9A from the CD-ROM here.

First, Abraham must acknowledge his legal status (v. 4): "I am an alien and a stranger." Since this was his legal standing, he was not permitted to purchase land without the consent of the whole community!

Display visual 9B from the CD-ROM here.

Second, the Hittites, a people originally from the area of today's Turkey, would properly address a man of Abraham's stature with the title (v. 6) *prince* or *lord.*

Display visual 9C from the CD-ROM here.

Third, the code of hospitality toward a guest of such importance required flowery language. Exaggeration and overstatement were understood as appropriate! For example, one could offer the property as a gift (v. 11), but everyone knew this was just polite conversation. Abraham properly responds before the whole community. This public discussion, so unlike our private business deals, was a legal requirement for a valid transaction. Abraham designates the property he seeks and calls for negotiations with its owner.

Display visual 9D from the CD-ROM here.

After the pleasantries and legal protocol, the hard bargaining begins! Abraham offers to buy the cave of Machpelah, which is (v. 9) "at the end of his field" for the full price. Ephron quickly counters (v. 11) with an offer to give his prospective buyer the field and the cave that is in it. Tucked into what appears to be a generous and open-ended gift was a shrewd business move. Ephron, by saying he will give the *field* to Abraham, was politely and adroitly saying, "I won't sell the cave apart from the field! You'll have to buy both!" The economic motive behind Ephron's counteroffer was the fact that land was taxed according to larger parcels and plots. If Abraham had purchased *only* the cave, Ephron would still have to pay taxes on it *and* on the field in which it was located! Shrewdly, he offers Abraham the whole field.

Perhaps we should think of the sorts of claims and offers made today in the purchase of a new or used car. We are not unlike Ephron and Abraham! Our exaggerations often disguise an underlying set of assumptions that are subtle but understood by all.

Display visual 9E from the CD-ROM here.

Abraham agrees (vv. 12–13) to buy the *entire* field. This agreement provides the legal context for Ephron to offer his real price (vv. 14–15): four hundred shekels of silver. Most students of this period would view Ephron's price as exceedingly high. In all likelihood he relied on the immediacy of Abraham's need. He asked for top dollar! Abraham agrees and pays the full price (v. 16) "in the hearing of the Hittites." The text is stressing that all was done in a strictly legal fashion. The detailed description of the property with such specifics as (v. 17) "all the trees" was also typical of the legal pattern of the day.

The stress (vv. 17–20) on the deeding of the land to Abraham and the public nature of that final exchange complete the picture. Every i is dotted and every t is crossed for the Hittite attorney!

2 Marriage: The Second Passage (Genesis 24)

Chapter 24 opens with a beautiful panorama of Abraham's life (v. 1): "Abraham was now old and well advanced in years, and the LORD had blessed him in every way." The blessing announced in Genesis 12:2–3 has remained over Abraham. As Abraham reflects in good old age, his thoughts turn to the heart of that blessing—his seed, Isaac. The patriarch ponders the lifeline, the messianic lifeline! Abraham's line will continue through Isaac. It is crucial that Isaac have an appropriate wife.

Aware of his age, Abraham calls his chief servant. By means of a solemn oath (v. 9), the servant assures his master that his request will be followed. If oaths are sometimes frivolous in our culture, the world of the patriarchs attached total allegiance and loyalty to them. Not only in Palestine, but in Egypt and elsewhere, it was assumed that one would die rather than break a sacred oath before God. Abraham (v. 7) encourages his servant with the assurance that the angel of the Lord will go before him and guarantee success.

Display visual 9F from the CD-ROM here.

From this point on we are treated to a delightful story of love and marriage. The servant leaves (v. 10) with 10 camels and "all kinds of good things" from his master. The custom of showering a prospective bride and her family with gifts is clearly in view. The servant was prepared!

Positioning himself near the town well at evening, the servant gained the maximum opportunity for meeting eligible maidens. Verses 12–14 record a touching prayer for God's presence. The servant sets up a test by which God can show "kindness" toward Abraham. The girl who not only draws water for the servant, but offers to water his camels as well, will be the girl God intended for Isaac. This is quite a different test from those offered by today's matchmaking services!

The text stresses the spontaneous nature of God's answer (v. 15): "Before he had finished praying, Rebekah came out with her jar on her shoulder." There is no polite beating around the bush in this meeting at the well. The God who created male and female highlights the goodness of this created order. Rebekah (v. 15) was from the right family. She (v. 16) was very beautiful. She was a virgin. The servant (v. 17) hurries to meet her. His faithfulness to his oath and eagerness to achieve its end are obvious. Rebekah's spontaneous response (vv. 18–19) suggests a scene that is postcard perfect. The twilight of the day, the cool of a desert evening, the simple beauty of women drawing water for their homes—all these combined under the hand of God to seal another generation of the messianic lifeline.

How frequently Rebekah and Isaac must have told others the story of how they met! This match was literally made in heaven! The text repeatedly stresses God's agency (vv. 27, 35, 42, 48). The immediate blessing (vv. 50–51) bestowed by Laban and Bethuel underscores the clarity of God's hand: "Laban and Bethuel answered, 'This is from the LORD; we can say nothing to you one way or the other. Here is Rebekah; take her and go, and let her become the wife of your master's son, as the LORD has directed.'"

Even after this moment, the humanity of all the participants shines through. On one hand, the servant is eager (v. 54) to be on his way the next morning. He's eager to complete his assignment. On the other hand, Rebekah's family (v. 55) wants to bid her a proper farewell. They request 10 days to enjoy her company prior to the painful moment of departure. Finally, Rebekah herself is called. Her willingness (v. 58) to go immediately sends the group on its way (v. 60) with a standard familial blessing.

This narrative builds quickly toward a climax! Isaac's sighting (v. 63) of the camels, Rebekah's (v. 64) first glimpse of Isaac, and her (v. 65) maidenly use of the veil all set the scene for a grand and touching summary. "Isaac (v. 67) brought her into the tent of his mother Sarah, and he married Rebekah. So she became his wife, and he loved her; and Isaac was comforted after his mother's death." Sarah had died, but the Lord's promise had not. Rebekah took her place in Sarah's tent and thus, symbolically, in the messianic lifeline that would now continue through Isaac and Rebekah.

3 A Second Death: The Final Passage (Genesis 25:1–11)

The comfort Rebekah brought to bring Isaac soon covered not only his mother's but also his father's death. Chapter 25, after briefly describing Abraham's marriage to Keturah, moves to his death.

As Genesis 25 begins, the text confirms Isaac as Abraham's rightful heir. Elsewhere in Scripture, Keturah is called a "concubine" (Genesis 25:6; 1 Chronicles 1:32). This term indicates a wife of lower status than Sarah. Abraham (Genesis 25:6) gave the sons of his lesser wives gifts and sent them away. This would insure Isaac's place as Abraham's only legal heir. Abraham's other sons would receive the blessing of the Lord for Abraham's sake. Yet, as the Lord had promised, Isaac would carry on Abraham's family line, the lifeline from which the Messiah would be born.

The text of Genesis 25:7–11 describes almost matter-of-factly the last days of a great patriarch. The reader longs for more detail. But the sentences are crisp and concise. "Altogether, Abraham lived a hundred and seventy-five years. Then Abraham breathed his last and died at a good old age, an old man and full of years; and he was gathered to his people" (vv. 7–8). This phrase ("gathered to his people"), later on repeated for Isaac and Jacob, is a euphemism for death, something like our euphemism "passed away." However, "gathered to one's people" expresses a beautiful hope in continuing life with the Lord and with other believers in eternity. What began with God's promise in Genesis 12 is now on its way to fulfillment in Genesis 25. Even Abraham's death now seems an appropriate passage to another age on God's lifeline. Not violence. Not an accident. But the fullness and completion of life are the accents that mark Abraham's death. The birth of Isaac, a large family, prosperity, and now burial with Sarah in the land that God had promised: all these features of Abraham's life point to God's presence and blessing.

Display visual 9G from the CD-ROM here.

The story of the life and death of Abraham, with all its passages, is more than merely this patriarch's personal history. It is, for those who see clearly, a story of our covenant Lord and His way with humanity. That way, so transparent in Abraham's life, is the way of grace. The Lord's self-disclosure, His gift of Himself, and His gracious presence are seen preeminently in Isaac's birth and life. And that birth was to alert God's people that His grace seeks concrete expression. Abraham's seed would lead to the birth that displays God's grace for all ages: the birth of Jesus Christ—Abraham's Savior and ours!

Concluding Activities

Speak a prayer thanking God for His blessing on this LifeLight course. Commend all participants to His continued blessing. Close with an expression of thanks to participants and leaders. Announce the next LifeLight course.

Notes

Small-Group Leaders Material

Genesis: The Beginning of Life and Light

Preparing for the Session

Central Focus

Because this is an introductory lesson, the focus is as much on the group as it is on the Book of Genesis. Questions are geared toward introducing Genesis while welcoming LifeLight participants.

Objectives

That the participant, as a child of God and with the Holy Spirit's help, will be led to

1. see a connection between God's purposes for creation and His purposes for our daily life;

2. grasp the primary purpose of all Scripture, including the purpose of Genesis;

3. understand the basic subject matter covered in the Book of Genesis;

4. contribute to a sense of rapport and commitment among the members of the LifeLight group.

For the Small-Group Leader

Because of the introductory nature of the material and the diversity of Bible knowledge among participants, the questions in this week's leaflet immediately lead learners into Scripture, but not too heavily. Emphasize establishing relationships during this first session.

Subsequent lessons in this course will be challenging. After all, this is in-depth Bible study. Stress this to your group. If they do not discipline themselves to set aside time each day to do the daily lessons, they will fall behind, become frustrated, and possibly drop out. Life-Light material aims to show how Scripture interprets Scripture. Therefore, many questions have one or two cross-references to assist participants in finding answers and to aid you in facilitating discussion. You will not have time to read the verses referenced in the study leaflets during the discussion sessions. Students will need to read these on their own before class.

Some questions are intended to encourage discussion. In some cases there may be no one correct answer. All scriptural references in the study questions are based on the New International Version (NIV) of the Bible, which may affect the answers to some questions.

Pray regularly for and with your LifeLight group; God will grant you fruitful times together in the Word!

Small-Group Discussion Helps

At this and the following discussion sessions you may bring this guide with you. As you read the discussion helps in preparation for the session, underline comments you want to share with the group during class time. Also jot notes to yourself in the margin. As the discussion proceeds, you will have both the study leaflet and the leaders guide turned to the discussion helps for that session. Remember that your goal is not to be the expert but the discussion leader—one who keeps the discussion moving and encourages and assists all group members to take part in the discussion. Study questions are numbered sequentially for the week so that any one question may be located quickly and easily.

If this is the first session of a new group, spend some time in getting acquainted. Distribute name tags as participants arrive. A fun, nonthreatening way to learn first names quickly: Ask each participant to think of a positive adjective that begins with the same sound as his or her first name. Introduce yourself with such an adjective—e.g., Adorable Agnes, Willing William, Electrifying Earl, Tall Ted, Marvelous Martha. Then ask the person at your left to repeat your adjective and name and add his or her own adjective and name: "This is Electrifying Earl, and I'm Joyful Judy." The next person in the circle repeats these two names and adds his or her own. When the circle of names is complete, the group may repeat all the names, one more time, in unison. (If your group is fairly large, repeat this name game in the session next time and in sessions thereafter until participants have learned each other's names.)

In addition to learning names, you may want to ask group members to tell the others something about themselves—their families, occupations, special interests, memorable experiences, or other information they may wish to share. Since getting acquainted is an important goal for this session, you may want to spend some time at this.

Day 1 • Genesis 1

1. This begins a series of questions about "purpose"—purpose for the universe, for Scripture, and for our personal lives. (a) The sun, moon, and stars were created for three purposes: to separate day from night, to provide signs to mark the seasons (more about that in next week's lesson), and to give light to the earth. (b) People were created to subdue and rule creation. (c) Plants were created for food.

2. By being created to do good works, we continue the creative activity of God as His representatives in this world. We not only are His workmanship but also His workers. *Note:* Ephesians 2:10 should never be read outside its context of Ephesians 2:8–9, lest someone assume we are saved by those good works.

3. Each of us was created to glorify God—even in common activities such as eating and drinking. Martin Luther said that the unbeliever sins when he eats breakfast. Why? Because he doesn't thank and glorify God for that meal. Explore some day-to-day activities of your fellow class members and how those activities can be used to glorify God. One of the best ways to glorify God is to share with others His name and His glorious plan for our salvation, as the Great Commission of Matthew 28 emphasizes.

4. The Bible is not a rule book. Rather, the Bible is a guide book pointing us to the Savior. During the discussion period use every textual opportunity to point to Jesus, the Messiah.

5. In 2 Timothy 3:16–17 we read that Scripture is useful for teaching (imparting knowledge), rebuking (reproving wrong behavior or wrong belief), correcting (pointing the way to godly living), training in righteousness (describing the right standing with God we have received in Jesus and that empowers righteous thoughts, words, and actions). When God's Word has done its holy work in us, we will be thoroughly equipped (ready and able, by grace) for every good work.

Day 2 • Genesis 1; Matthew 1

6. **Challenge question.** *Genesis* means "origins" or "beginnings." Genesis traces the "family tree" of all believers, as it were. Matthew knew how important that family tree of Jesus was to the Jews, because it led all the way back to King David and even to Abraham, the father of the Jews, from whom the Messiah would come. Much of Genesis will be about Abraham, to whom that covenant promise of a Savior was given.

7. (a) Genesis 3:15 gives the first promise of a Savior. (b) Genesis 4:1–2 tells of Adam and Eve's first two children, who became the world's first shepherd (Abel) and the world's first farmer (Cain). (c) Genesis 4:8 records the world's first murder. (d) Genesis 4:20 describes Jabal, who was the first nomadic herdsman. (e) Genesis 4:21 tells of Jubal, the first musician and, possibly, instrument maker. (f) Genesis 4:22 records Tubal-Cain, the first blacksmith. (g) Genesis 11:1–7 tells about the first city, the first "skyscraper," and the genesis of the world's different languages.

8. Moses' honesty may surprise us. Perhaps we would have downplayed the sins of the Bible's characters. But Scripture never does. It depicts human sin in all its disgusting details. The hero—the *only* hero—of the Bible is our Lord. Like Adam, Eve, Sarah, Jacob, and all the rest, we too are sinners. But even as God's grace in Christ overflowed to His people of old, so too it overflows to us!

9. The promise of the Messiah to Adam, Noah, Abraham, and the other patriarchs, including Judah, through whose tribe the Savior would come, is a vital part of Genesis and of world history. If we had no record of the fall into sin, how would we fully know of our need for the forgiveness of sins?

Day 3 • Selected texts

10. Although this question asks for an opinion, a brief outline of the highlights of Genesis will assist those who

are not familiar with the book. The study leaflet contains a thematic outline from the *Concordia Self-Study Bible*.

11. (a) Let volunteers share. Subdivision covenants detail the responsibilities homeowners agree to respect. Let participants share other instances of this word's use today. Point out that usually covenants are reciprocal; each party agrees to keep up his or her end of the bargain. (b) In Genesis 9:8–17 the Lord makes an unconditional, one-sided covenant never to destroy the earth by flood again. In Genesis 17:1–11 He makes an unconditional covenant with Abram. While circumcision serves as a sign and seal of this covenant, it does not benefit God in any way. It simply reminds Abram (later "Abraham") of the Lord's saving love. Genesis 26:23–25 records the Lord's reaffirmation of Abraham's covenant to his son Isaac. Genesis 35:9–15 tells of the Lord's repetition of the covenant promise to Isaac's son Jacob. So we see the covenant pass from Abraham to Isaac to Jacob with no strings attached. The promises carried no conditions. (c) **Challenge question.** Galatians 3:26–29 tells us that all those who believe in Christ belong to Christ. Through faith (v. 26) we have become "Abraham's seed" (v. 29) and heirs of the covenant promises Abraham himself inherited. Baptism marks us as heirs, just as circumcision marked Abraham and his descendants.

Day 4 • Selected verses from Genesis

12. (a) Let participants comment on ways they see time as a blessing. Time makes history and, in one sense, meaning possible here on earth. It reminds us of our limitations, our creatureliness and therefore helps us look upon the eternal God with awe. (b) Before sin infected God's creation, the Lord gave Adam work. God intended that it be a blessing, not a curse. Though because of sin work has become harder and at times monotonous or dangerous, from the beginning, the Lord intended it to bring His human creatures joy and meaning. (c) **Challenge question.** Discuss this as a group. By obeying God's command regarding the tree of the knowledge of good and evil, Adam and Eve could worship Him, could demonstrate that their Creator meant more to them than the material things He creat-

ed. Some scholars believe Eve was worshiping at the tree when Satan came to her in Genesis 3:1. (d) Let group members share.

Day 5 • Selected verses from Genesis

13. (a) Point to the mention of the Spirit in Genesis 1:2 and to the mix of singular and plural pronouns in Genesis 1:26–28. (b) The serpent is portrayed as crafty and deceitful. He throws God's word and God's goodness into question. Neither his methods nor his character have changed through the ages. (c) The cherubim (plural) obey God's commands and have a kind of power unavailable to human beings. In Genesis 3:24 they serve as guardians. These facts recur throughout Scripture. (d) In Genesis 3:21 another first occurs—the first sacrifice. Here God Himself kills animals to clothe Adam and Eve. This "shedding of blood" foreshadows the entire sacrificial system instituted at Sinai. More importantly, it foreshadows the death of God's own Son on the cross. By that sacrifice in our place Jesus removed our sin and its shame forever!

The Lifeline Grows

Genesis 1–2

Preparing for the Session

Central Focus

This lesson focuses on a God who is both powerful and personal, whose awesome Word brought our entire universe into existence, and whose personal touch shaped clay into a man and formed a rib into a woman. Genesis 1 (the more general account of creation) emphasizes God's power, while Genesis 2 (which expands the details about the creation of man) emphasizes His personal touch.

Objectives

That the participant, as a child of God and with the Holy Spirit's help, will be led to

1. marvel at God's almighty power and wisdom in His plan of creation;

2. understand the position of human beings in God's plan of creation;

3. understand the God-intended unique relationship between male and female;

4. grow in a sense of stewardship by examining the components of the creation account.

For the Small-Group Leader

Different students will devote different amounts of time to their study at home, but they need to be encouraged to complete their lessons, for their own sakes as well as for the sake of their discussion group. The account of the creation is packed with insights for our application today. It will take us into some areas that are controversial, such as creation and evolution and the relative roles of male and female. Put your heart into this lesson! God's Spirit will open your heart to an array of personal applications as you meditate on His Word!

Think about ways to pace the flow of discussion as you move through the study leaflet questions. Some questions are intended as mere fact-finding questions. These draw students into the biblical material. You will need to spend little time on these questions in the group setting. Other questions, however, are purposely speculative and do not always have a right or wrong answer. They are intended to help students think more deeply about the material and its application.

From time to time, this section of leaders helps will include some hints to help you deal with group members and their situations. For example, what can you do with the person who loves to talk and talk? First, consider the reason for the talkativeness. Does a sense of personal insecurity lead the individual to overcompensate verbally? Or perhaps the individual lacks the organizational skills required to state opinions concisely. Whatever the reason, avoid embarrassing the participant. Instead, try to guide the conversation in such a way that others have opportunities to take part also. In some cases you may have to interrupt by saying, "That's an interesting point, so let's quickly see how some of the other members of our group feel about it before we go on to our next study question."

Small-Group Discussion Helps

Review question: With God's promise of the woman's Seed ("offspring"—NIV) who would crush the serpent's head, God set into motion His plan for our salvation—a plan that would find its fulfillment in the coming of Jesus. The entire Old Testament presents a lifeline that reaches its climax in Jesus.

Day 1 • Genesis 1:1–8

1. Ask your group if they ever made a cake from scratch. Then ask them if they grew the wheat or raised the chicken that laid the eggs that went into the cake! God created the world *ex nihilo* (Latin meaning "out of nothing"), without raw materials. The Hebrew word stem *qal* ("create") is used exclusively for God's activity. Therefore, the only true creations come from God, not human beings.

2. The Hebrew word used in Genesis 1:1–8 for God is *Elohim*. It's a plural noun in form, but yet, as here, indicates a singular subject. There is one true God, yet three persons. John 1:1 is a clear tie-in with Genesis 1:1 and explicitly calls the Son the Word. God the Word is distinct from God the Father ("with God") and yet is completely and fully God ("was God"). God's speaking words as He creates (1:3) points to the Word, the second person of the Trinity. The Spirit hovering (1:2) points to the third person of the Trinity. Genesis 1:26 may be taken either as a reference to the three persons consulting together or as an instance of the "divine we"—God speaking as the Creator-King.

3. (a) Nature, at best, reveals that there is a God, but only Scripture reveals the true God. With your group explore which attributes of God are revealed simply by looking at the created world (almighty, orderly, patient, etc.). (b) God's forgiving love—and the giving of His Son, Jesus—could never be figured out just by examining nature.

4. (a) Unlike the deist's "great clock maker" god who creates but refuses to intervene in maintaining his creation, the triune God sustains everything. In the spiritual realm, He sustains the faith that His Spirit has created in us. (b) How? He sustains our faith through Bible study, public worship services, the Lord's Supper, and our speaking the Word to one another. Whenever God touches us in any way with His Word, that Word strengthens our faith, sustaining it. In the physical realm, He gives us all we need for this body and life.

5. God not only brings people's sins to light so they might repent, but He even gives them the ability to know the Savior, thus leading them from the kingdom of darkness into the kingdom of light (1 Peter 2:9).

6. (a) "And there was evening, and there was morning." (b) In Exodus 20:11 the use of the numerical adjective before the word for "day" strongly indicates literal, 24-hour days.

Day 2 • Genesis 1:9–25

7. The calming of the storm in Mark 4 recognizes Jesus as Lord of the universe. Now consider all the storms Jesus has calmed in your life. Be still and know that He is God.

8. Plant life soon would sustain animal life.

9. The text says their purpose is to separate day from night, to mark the seasons, and to give light to the earth. Other passages tell us that the heavenly luminaries (a) encourage and affirm faith; (b) help forecast the weather; (c) provide prophetic signs; and (d) signal the coming judgment.

10. Only the Creator is in control of His creation. Giving the Creator's glory to His created things is foolish and futile.

11. (a) God knows them all, counts each of them. (b) Some people—for fear of bothering God—are afraid to ask Him for what they consider to be insignificant things. However, God is concerned about every detail of our lives.

12. The Hebrew word for "according to its kind" does not demand a separate creation by God of each species, but it does require the separate creation of families within orders.

Day 3 • Genesis 1:26–2:3

13. Human beings were meant to share in exercising lordship, rule, and dominion over the earth.

14. Although in Baptism the Holy Spirit gives us the new self, patterned after God in righteousness, and calls us to be saints even now, it is not until the day of resurrection that our bodies will be totally free of the old sinful nature and fully restored to the original image of God.

15. Although any answer is speculative, God's original command concerning population growth must be considered from the perspective of an empty earth and, ultimately, in the context of people's responsibility to be good stewards of an earth that is no longer empty.

16. Because no mention is made of carnivores in Genesis 1, perhaps God did intend for us to order from a vegetarian menu. Nevertheless, sin changed much about God's original plan. While we walk this sin-changed world, God does not forbid the eating of meat or demand kosher eating habits so long as we see our food

as coming from God's bounty and thank Him for it.

17. The formation of light on day 1 is completed with the luminaries of day 4. The water formed under and above the expanse (day 2) is filled with the teeming creatures of day 5. Formation of the seas, dry land, and vegetation on day 3 is completed by the creation on days 5 and 6 of living creatures to dwell in the land and seas and to eat the plants for food.

18. (a) God is almighty and needs no rest ("rest" here means simply that He stopped creating), (b) but finite man does—for physical and spiritual refreshment. God's rest reminds us of *our* need for this refreshment. This is especially so since the fall into sin. Now we need the refreshment of the Gospel. Ultimately, the place of complete rest is in heaven. On this earth, God's people rest in Jesus, our Savior from sin. God's rest on the seventh day also directs us toward that eternal rest.

19. This is a good opportunity for the group members to share their faith. Let volunteers comment, but don't pressure anyone to respond.

Day 4 • Genesis 2:4–17

20. Water is used for cleansing and for consumption. Christ is the living water because He washes all of our sins away (giving us the gift of eternal life) and because He refreshes and nourishes us with this water of life. Because Christ is eternal, the living water will never stop refreshing us.

21. Specially formed from the ground, man is given dominion over the animals (as the naming process indicates). Because both humans and animals are God's creation, we have the duty to respect all life.

22. Encourage the group to use its creativity. Think in terms of climate, communication, work, and so forth.

23. Peter describes (2 Peter 3:13) "a new heaven and a new earth." Such an environment might be similar to the original Eden! Down through history some doctrinal errors minimized or even denigrated the value of the physical universe. Yet Scripture clearly teaches that we will enjoy perfect physical bodies in heaven. Our heavenly existence will not be only spiritual, but will take place on a physical plane. Jesus Himself has a glorified, physical body. One day, so will we!

24. A truly free will allows the option of opposing God's will. God created no robots, but rather He made children—human beings with a free will. Adam and Eve could love and obey God because they wanted to, not because they had to.

25. **Challenge question.** Satan, not God, tempted Eve. Satan intended to destroy the faith of God's human children. God, on the other hand, gave His children the gifts of worship and of free will in planting the tree of the knowledge of good and evil in Eden. Refer to session 1, question 12c and its designated answer, and consult your pastor if group members need further help in answering this question.

Day 5 • Genesis 2:18–25

26. Perhaps *helper* is still the best way to describe this ideal, uniquely corresponding individual who, unlike the animals but very much like God, is able to empathize with man and help him.

27. This happens not only sexually but also emotionally and spiritually. The reformer Martin Luther said, "Christians get married in order to help each other to heaven." Marriage unifies the goals of two people.

28. Children always owe honor, respect, and loving care to their parents, even if those children are married. However, parents must realize that apron strings are meant to be only so long and that a new family unit arises with the marriage of a child. Accept reasonable responses that reflect these principles.

29. **Challenge question.** Your group should be able to select the psalmist's parallels to the creation of light, the separation of the water and the land, the references to various categories of animal life, man's relationship to work, food, the breath of life, and so forth.

30. Answers may include references to His almighty power, love, orderliness, holiness, and patience.

The Lifeline Is Cut—and Restored

Genesis 3–5

Preparing for the Session

Central Focus

These chapters of Genesis are a study of a good world gone bad. Relationships deteriorate quickly as sin appears and works its way through the world. In these chapters also we find the origin of two kinds of people—one line descended from Cain and the other descended from Seth. They are two branches of the same family tree, both talented. But one, though infected by sin, looks in faith for a Savior, while the other continues on a course of rebellion, arrogance, and violence that moves God to bring down the ax of judgment.

Objectives

That the participant, as a child of God and with the Holy Spirit's help, will be led to

1. recognize God's grace even as the curse of sin falls on the entire human race;

2. understand the God-intended relationships between God, His human creatures, and the world;

3. appreciate the believer's position as a member of God's family and of the line of promise.

For the Small-Group Leader

Perhaps you have already discovered that your group includes someone who seems particularly argumentative. If so, work to prevent the discussion from deteriorating into an argument. Attempt to find merit in one of the points this person is making and then move quickly to another topic. As a last resort you may have to speak with the individual privately.

Small-Group Discussion Helps

Review Question: People are the peak of God's creative work, the highpoint of God's creative activity.

Day 1 • Genesis 3:1–13

1. The Isaiah and Revelation passages combine to identify Satan as the creature who entered into a serpent in the garden. Because he and the other demons effectively continue to use the same strategy to tempt people today, believers need to be aware of this technique in order to combat it. (a) First, Satan cast seeds of doubt when he said to Eve, "Did God really say, 'You must not eat from any tree in the garden'?" Next he contradicted God's Word when he told her, "You will not surely die." Finally, Satan extended a treacherous promise of his own when he said, "For God knows that when you eat of it your eyes will be opened, and you will be like God, knowing good and evil."

(b) Because pride lay at the root of Satan's fall (he, an angelic creature, wanted to assume the Creator's authority), James 4:7 warns us that we must first humble ourselves before God in order to obtain His power to resist the devil. John 8:44 warns us never to accept the words of Satan or of his followers at face value. Luke 4 demonstrates that the only effective weapon against the father of lies is the truth, God's inspired and inerrant Word.

2. Eve viewed the fruit (we do not know what kind of fruit it was) as "good for food" even though it was forbidden (the lust of the flesh). She also saw the fruit as "pleasing to the eye" (the lust of the eyes), and "desirable for gaining wisdom," a wisdom she felt God was withholding from her (the pride of life).

3. We cannot hide our thoughts or actions from an omniscient God. But each time we fail to confess our sins to God or try to cover up before our neighbor, we are, in effect, attempting to hide from God's presence, just like Jonah (Jonah 1:1–3) or the unbelievers at the Last Day (Revelation 6:15–16). Instead of basking in God's presence, the guilt of sin found Adam and Eve trembling in fear behind the bushes.

4. The purpose of this divine interrogation process is to provide the opportunity for God's children to repent willingly. Example: A mother asks her son if he has been eating her freshly baked cookies (even though she sees crumbs all over his face), although she had told him earlier not to eat any of them. Her question gives the child an opportunity to acknowledge his misdeed.

5. (a) Adam blames God as much as he blames Eve, since it was God's decision to give him the woman! (b) Eve blames the serpent, even though the serpent was merely a mask of Satan. (c) God holds Adam accountable. Eve may be responsible for taking the first bite (1 Timothy 2:11–15), but Adam is ultimately held responsible as the representative of the entire human race. (d) Nevertheless, it is Jesus who takes the full responsibility for our sins—including the original sin—upon Himself.

Day 2 • Genesis 3:14–24

6. The results of the first sin demonstrate that everything man does has consequences that may stretch even beyond human boundaries. Plant life became subject to the whimsy of man's poor stewardship and the ravages of the weather, while the animal world quickly learned to fear the human beings who had once protected them.

7. **Challenge question.** The serpent (Satan) wounds the offspring (the Savior) with the bite of death, but—as in killing a serpent—the head or authority of Satan is permanently crushed under the weight of the resurrected Savior.

8. (a and b) Work was originally a blessing because it reflected the creative aspect of the image of God. Work itself is certainly not a curse. Nevertheless, work—like other aspects of creation—bears the consequences of sin and may become drudgery or stressful.

9. **Challenge question.** While the Bible does not tell us why God replaced the covering of fig leaves Adam and Eve had made for themselves with a covering of animal skins He made for them, this act implies the sacrifice of atonement, made by the shedding of Christ's blood on the cross, which covers our sins. Christ's sacrifice was also foreshadowed by the animal sacrifices required in the Old Testament (Hebrews 9:13–14).

10. God gives the reason He expelled Adam and Eve from the garden after their sin in verse 22. In His mercy God saw to it that people would be prevented from living forever in the misery of sin's curse, the curse they had brought on themselves by their sin. Death would put an end to the sinful human nature and our miserable existence on this earth, corrupted by sin. God devised a plan by which our sin might be covered and we might have a new life, free of sin, enjoyed in a new paradise where we might eat the tree of life and live forever in bliss (Revelation 2:7).

11. Sin is the rebellion of our very being, even before it has acted in deeds. It is putting our own desires before God's will.

Day 3 • Genesis 4:1–16

12. (a) Because God looks at the heart, it was faith that made Abel's gift acceptable and lack of faith that made Cain's gift unacceptable. (b) Genesis 4:4 points out that Abel brought God the best (the fat portions) from the firstborn of his flock. Cain brought "some of the fruits of the soil." Furthermore, Cain's ready anger suggests he brought his offering resentfully. (c) Do not ask participants to share their answers to this part of the question.

13. Answers may be as secular as "counting to 10" or as sacred as confession followed by prayers for strength. Others may seek the encouragement and advice of fellow Christians. Still others may find their strength to combat their temptation in their participation in Bible study. Stress the truth that God wants to help us; He provides the strength we need through his Word and the Sacraments.

14. (a, b, and c) The Matthew passages reinforce our concern for others in thought, word, and deed—treating them as we would treat Christ Himself. Accept specific examples based on the Matthew 5 text.

15. **Challenge question.** Both were the innocent blood of prophets but, while Abel's blood cries out with vengeance, Jesus' blood speaks the better word of forgiveness that washes away our sins.

16. (a) Point out that God often is unduly gracious to those who have rejected Him. (b) Then ask your group

for possible reasons. Peter tells us of God's great desire to bring everyone to repentance.

Day 4 • Genesis 4:17–26

17. Through Moses God forbade marriage to a sister (Leviticus 18:6, 9). In the case of Cain, however, this prohibition was not yet in effect; in fact, Cain would have had to marry a sister since his father, Adam, was the father of all people (Acts 17:26). History traces the rise of technology and the decline of morality. Today's advanced armaments produce more efficient ways of killing more people. Medical advances lead to bioethical dilemmas that appall Christians. Accept other examples that illustrate the process begun in Genesis 4:17–24.

18. Procreation was not the primary purpose of marriage; otherwise, God might have used several of Adam's ribs! Christ's words in Matthew 19:4–6 make God's original, monogamous plan very clear. Polygamy may produce more offspring, but it also breeds jealousy, pride, lust, and other undesirable traits.

19. Only God, the giver of life, has the right to avenge life. Lamech assumed an even greater authority than God. God said He would avenge potential killers of Cain 7 times over, but Lamech claimed he would avenge himself 77 times. Instead, Matthew 18:21–22 shows us that believers are schooled in a different form of multiplication—*forgiveness* 77 times over.

20. The birth of Seth brought comfort to Eve, who mourned the murder of Abel. The greater comfort, however, is that Seth's line would eventually produce the Savior of the world, Jesus Christ.

21. Until that time worship had been individual and spontaneous. Genesis, the book of origins, here relates the origin of our modern worship services. We need corporate worship to support and encourage each other in the faith, but we also need personal quiet time with the Lord to read and listen to Him in the Word as He speaks to our lives. Choosing one kind of worship over the other is detrimental to our faith life. The Spirit can best work in our hearts when we combine both public and personal worship.

Day 5 • Genesis 5

22. In that godly list is the name of righteous Noah, who would be God's agent in sparing the world from total annihilation and from whose line the Messiah would come.

23. (a) The phrase "and then he died" recurs down through the genealogy. (b) Enoch was translated into heaven alive. We believers who are alive when the Last Day comes will have a similar experience (1 Thessalonians 4:17–18).

24. The call to discipleship is to follow in Christ's footsteps. The patriarchs occasionally strayed off the path of faith, just as we do, but as we rely on the Holy Spirit's wisdom and strength—not our own—we also can follow in the steps that Enoch trod.

The Lifeline Is Narrowed

Genesis 6–10

Preparing for the Session

Central Focus

The study of Noah and the ark is one of the Bible's definitive examples of how God can be just and merciful at the same time. Although our natural curiosity makes it tempting to dwell on the catastrophic elements of the flood account, the most important aspect of this story is how God lovingly and patiently protects a righteous remnant so that the lifeline to a Messiah can continue.

Objectives

That the participant, as a child of God and with the Holy Spirit's help, will be led to

1. understand that God must punish sin;

2. rejoice in God's patience in dealing with sinners;

3. see God's covenant protection in our lives today;

4. discover the genealogical roots of our civilization.

For the Small-Group Leader

You will discover that there are more questions than can be asked and more information than can realistically be furnished when dealing with the flood account. Many fine books are available in Christian bookstores to assist lay people who wish to learn more about the flood. By comparing some of the accounts of the great flood written by ancient pagans, one also gains a greater appreciation for the truth of the events recorded in Genesis 6–8. Due to the awesome, cataclysmic nature of the flood, it may be tempting to let the discussion major in minors. Instead, keep the flow of conversation directed to a merciful God who continues to seek out and save those who seek after righteousness and claim His promises through faith in Christ Jesus.

Small-Group Discussion Helps

Review question: Proceeding from Adam and Eve were the ungodly line of Cain and the godly line of Seth. Through Seth would come the lifeline leading to the Savior.

Day 1 • Genesis 6

1. (a) The Savior would be born to a believing remnant. If no believers were alive on earth, the gracious plan of God would have been thwarted. Later, God prohibited the Jews from intermarrying with other nations so Israel would not be led away from their unique role of producing the Savior, who would save the world from sin. With the Savior's coming, this prohibition had served its purpose. (b) Some believe that "sons of God" refers to angels and that the Nephilim were their superhuman progeny. But Jesus' words in Mark 12:25 speak against such an idea—angels do not procreate. Also, God's orders about reproducing in kind (Genesis 1:11–12, 21, 24) speak against this interpretation. However, the text leaves no question as to the moral condition of the world's population by describing it as wicked, evil, corrupt, and full of violence.

2. If Genesis 6:3 is a reference to shorter life spans, it was a gradual, yet nonetheless traceable process after the flood as demonstrated by subsequent genealogies. *Favor* (NIV) in verse 8 is the word for grace, its first use in Scripture. Ezekiel singles out Noah, Daniel, and Job as examples of righteousness. Your group may list a number of other biblical figures, such as Abraham and Paul.

3. Matthew 15:18–19 shows that everyone has a congenital heart ailment known as original sin (Psalm 51:5), causing each person inevitably to think, speak, and act out that sin. If this were not so, why has no one (except Jesus) in the history of civilization ever totally stopped sinning?

4. We all need to be faithful "preachers of righteousness" by word and example, particularly during these

end times (Hebrews 10:23, 25). However, we leave the results of our witness in God's hands.

5. It is said that a people that does not know its history is doomed to repeat it. Our generation goes on with its normal activities of marrying and burying, eating and drinking—just as in Noah's time—with the majority of people either oblivious to God's warnings or scoffing and ridiculing those who warn of a Judgment Day.

Day 2 • Genesis 7

6. Noah and his family were graciously declared righteous because of the faith God gave to them. The promises of God to all who believe create certainty in our hearts that the invitation to salvation has our names engraved on it.

7. The ratio was determined according to the eventual need of having kosher (clean) animals to eat and of having others to offer up as sacrifices to the Lord.

8. The waters of the flood covered all the mountains (7:19). It killed every living thing on the earth. Only Noah and those in the ark survived. The flood lasted over a year! An ark with nearly 100,000 square feet of deck space could hardly have been designed for a local flood. If the flood were not universal, why not simply flee to some place high and dry? Anything less than a universal flood could not have destroyed all of humankind, as God said He would do in Genesis 6:7. God vowed never to repeat the flood, so if it were local, He lied—there have been many local floods over the centuries. Jesus Himself says all people were destroyed in the flood (Luke 17:26–27).

9. They were in the ark slightly over a year!

Day 3 • Genesis 8

10. Do not press any members for an answer. However, those who might wish to share how God manifested His faithfulness and comforting presence to them after a traumatic loss or event will undoubtedly find sympathetic listeners, who will be able to relate that faithfulness to their own lives.

11. If our faith were not based on historical fact, it would be worthless. Archaeological discoveries constantly verify its historical reality and accuracy. But our faith resides in God's Word, God's promises, not in historical artifacts.

12. The answers to this question may separate the pessimists from the optimists. Some would see only devastation and rotting corpses, while others would see an opportunity to remake the world in God's image. The devastation would certainly have produced awe in Noah's heart as he considered the Lord's power. However, the grace of God in preserving a remnant through which the world's Savior would come also would have evoked awe and led to a desire to worship. Perhaps participants would also have experienced a deep sense of responsibility in starting the human race all over again. This may have led them to earnest prayer for the Lord's help and wisdom. Accept other responses drawn from the text.

13. God regarded the sacrifice literally with "a smell of satisfaction" and promised to maintain the cycle of seasons and never again to strike the earth with a universal flood. However, the ground, cursed by Adam's sin, retained that curse. Point out that God has been faithful to the promises He made that day. We can also take comfort in knowing that our obedience, empowered by Christ's life in us (John 15:5), still smells sweet to Him.

14. Only Christ's perfect life and death in our place makes our sacrifices acceptable.

Day 4 • Genesis 9:1–17

15. Animals would be afraid of humans (perhaps for our protection or perhaps due to our abuse of animals), and animals would become acceptable food for man. What a contrast to all the animals obediently coming to Adam in Genesis 2:19 to be named and to the dove finding safety in Noah's hand in Genesis 8:9!

16. (a) The flesh of animals was given for food, but the life of the flesh was in the blood (symbolic of life) and reserved for sacrifice (Leviticus 17:11). (b) Jesus gave His life for our redemption. That life is represented by the Savior's blood being poured out for us.

17. (a) The government is God's ordained agent of jus-

tice, (b) preventing the potential abuse of individual vengeance.

18. Still today the rainbow is a sign of God's promise that He will not again destroy the earth by a flood.

19. Fire.

20. The enrichment magazine that accompanies this course gives an excellent summary of various types of covenants, including the one with Noah. To seal a covenant with the believing descendants of Abraham, God gave circumcision as a sign. The Sabbath observance was a sign of the Lord's covenant with Moses and the Israelites. The water of Baptism is a sign of the covenant God has made with us. In each case, the power rests in the word and promise of God, not in the visible sign itself.

21. **Challenge question.** In both the flood and Baptism, it was God who did the saving, and it was done through the use of water. (Note to small-group leader: 1 Peter 3:18–19 refers to Christ's descent into hell after His death but before His resurrection to proclaim His victory on the cross over sin, death, and Satan.) The floodwaters that destroyed the ungodly were the means by which God saved Noah and his family. In Baptism the Holy Spirit works faith in Christ in our hearts. Believers are saved by what Baptism effects through Christ's death and resurrection.

....
Day 5 • Genesis 9:18–10:32

22. (a) Psalm 104:14–15 includes wine as a gift of God. Noah was not sinning in planting the vineyard or in drinking wine, but in drinking too much wine and becoming drunk. (b) Any of God's gifts has the potential of being abused by us. Therefore, we must learn how to give thanks for whatever we receive and to use it to God's glory.

23. (a) Ham exposed his father to ridicule; this was a sin against the commandment that requires us to honor our parents. (b) Shem and Japheth were motivated by love for their father when they removed the evidence of his shameful behavior from view.

24. These verses were once misrepresented to discriminate against African Americans, because the majority of Ham's line supposedly settled in the areas of Africa. However, Canaan's family, a part of Ham's line, settled in Palestine and were not African American. (a) Both Shem and Japheth were blessed, but Shem would receive the greater blessing. (b) Shem's line would worship the true God and would bring forth the Savior, in whom the descendants of Japheth (and Ham) would find redemption.

25. Linguistic corresponds to *languages*, political to *nations*, ethnic to *clans*, and geographical to *territories*.

26. Just as God shut the door of the ark, sealing Noah and his family safely inside, Jesus is a door or gate protecting us like the shepherd who lies down in the gateway to keep the sheep safe from wild animals. The psalmist and Isaiah also view the Lord as our refuge from the storms of life that try to overwhelm us.

The Lifeline Is Strengthened

Genesis 11–13

Preparing for the Session

Central Focus

Just as God saved Noah even while He executed judgment on sinful mankind, so God in His mercy called Abram from a world of proud pagans to carry on the line of promise.

Objectives

That the participant, as a child of God and with the Holy Spirit's help, will be led to

1. recognize the reasons for God's judgment on a world that sees no need for the true God;

2. praise God for His mercy showered on the world through the call of Abram;

3. rely on God's forgiveness through the world's Savior just as Abram did—by grace;

4. learn that through Abram's Descendant—Jesus—we also have been blessed to be a blessing.

Small-Group Discussion Helps

Review question: God's wrath was evident when He completely destroyed all living things on the earth by the flood. The only exceptions, Noah, his family, and the creatures with them on the ark, display God's grace shown in the same event.

Day 1 • Genesis 11:1–9

1. Moses inserts Genesis 11:1–9 to explain how the events of Genesis 10 came about. Then he goes on to describe the vitally important genealogical line of Shem (11:10–32), which will produce the Messiah. Linguists believe all known languages are related and come from a common origin. Genesis 10:10–12 not only tells us that Nimrod was a great builder, but that he was responsible for building Babylon, the area where the Tower of Babel was located.

2. Some believe as much as 1,000 years may have passed between the time of the flood and the Tower of Babel. Perhaps, but we know that human beings easily forget God's lessons even more quickly. Note the words *us, we,* and *ourselves* in verses 3–4. The people were attempting to insure their reputations as a great nation, and they wanted a one-world government to prevent them from scattering over the face of the globe, even though it would be a government that would undoubtedly slip into dictatorial rule and slavery for the people.

3. Humanity was to *fill* the earth, not huddle in one corner of it.

4. Our sinful nature tends to prepare the blueprints for all of our building projects. It designs even our most noble efforts and chisels away the godly parts until what remains bears a marked likeness to our own inflated egos.

5. This multistoried tower may have been intended for use as a citadel against enemy attack or even as high ground in case of another flood. But by comparing this ziggurat with others, it is most likely that it was used for pagan religious and occult practices—something clearly forbidden in Deuteronomy 18:10–13. Undoubtedly, God found *both* their pride and their paganism to be an abomination.

6. The verb *plan* (NIV) or *plot* in Genesis 11:6 and Psalm 2:1 is always used in Scripture to describe evil schemes created by human beings. Towers and cities cannot be built, nor can people live together in harmony, unless those concerned are understood by one another. The language confusion caused the dispersion. Evidently, some small groups were left to speak the same language or dialect, and they migrated to their own location.

7. Zephaniah looks to a time of "purified lips." The Pentecost miracle temporarily bridged the barriers of Babel by letting God's Word be spoken in many languages; even today Christians of all nationalities speak

with "one voice" in acknowledging Christ as Savior of all the nations.

Day 2 • Genesis 11:10–32

8. Abram ("exalted father") became Abraham ("father of many"); Sarai became Sarah ("princess").

9. The people of Ur knew geometry and could calculate square and cube roots. Thousands of clay writing tablets also have been discovered. These moon worshipers believed the new moon was the crescent-shaped boat the moon god Nanna sailed across the sky! Even the literal meanings of the names *Terah, Laban, Sarai,* and *Milcah* are connected to the moon god. (a) Acts 7 tells us that God appeared to Abram, commanding him to leave this environment and to go to a land God would show him. (b) Let participants comment. The Hebrews text points to the faith the Lord planted in Abram's heart. It tells us Abram did not know where he was going and that he lived as a foreigner throughout his life as he waited for a city that would be his permanent home, (v. 10) an eternal home—heaven.

Day 3 • Genesis 12:1–9

10. Abram's move probably meant losing his inheritance, as well as access to the wealth and sophistication of the wealthiest city of that day—all to live in a land he had never even seen!

11. Believers must be honest with themselves in admitting the struggle they undoubtedly would encounter. But the Lord promises to sustain His people in their godly decisions and give them all they need wherever He sends them.

12. The Lord promises Abram (a) "I will make you into a great nation"; (b) "I will bless you"; (c) "I will make your name great"; (d) "You will be a blessing"; (e) "I will bless those who bless you"; (f) "Whoever curses you I will curse"; (g) "All peoples on earth will be blessed through you."

13. (a) Through Abram's Descendant, Jesus, all people may know the God of Abram and receive the salvation Abram received through faith in the world's Redeemer. (b) The gift of faith with which God blessed us is also a blessing we can share with others.

14. Abram viewed earth as a temporary residence, but his relationship with God was to last forever. Answers to this question may refer to the upbringing of a Christian family, a life of witnessing to others about Jesus, a will with a Christian preamble, a scholarship fund to assist young people going into professional ministry, and so forth.

Day 4 • Genesis 12:10–20

15. During the patriarchal period, there were three major famines (Genesis 12:10; 26:1; 41:56). Palestinians were at the mercy of the November and December rains. Abram was not guided by direct revelation at every point of his life, but since no mention is made of prayer or requests for God's guidance, perhaps Abram's faith was weakening. After all, God had promised His blessing upon Abram. Otherwise, going to Egypt was not wrong, in and of itself.

16. Either Sarai loved Abram very much or she, too, failed to trust God's promise of provision and blessing.

17. No doubt Hagar, Sarai's Egyptian maidservant, was acquired while Abram dwelt in Egypt (12:16). Hagar would become a means by which Abram and Sarai acted on their distrust of God's promises, and she was later a source of conflict in Abram's household (16:4–6; 21:8–11).

18. (a) Both must be held accountable for their reprehensible policies. Abram, however, knew God and was called to trust God to protect him. (b) This question is for personal reflection only. You may ask volunteers to share what helps them with trusting God in vulnerable times. God's Word and the Sacraments are our refuge in times of temptation and doubt. Point out that often it helps to pour out our hearts to another believer so that person can speak God's Word to us, personalizing it to our situation. We do this for one another in a spirit of humility, recognizing that we, too, are vulnerable. Next time, we ourselves may need the comfort and support.

Day 5 • Genesis 13

19. Abram "called on the name of the LORD" at Bethel, a place where he had built an altar. Bethel would play an important role in Abram's future.

20. (a) Abram proposed that he and Lot separate so quarrels between their herdsmen might be avoided. (b) By right Abram had first choice since God had given the land to Abram and to his descendants (Lot was a nephew), but Abram chose not to assert this right.

21. Complaints and arguments give a poor Christian witness, while a humble, gentle, patient, and loving attitude promotes peace and unity. A generous spirit will also see the blessings of that generosity returned to the giver in one way or another. Even if this were not so, it would be better to be wronged than to wrong someone else. It was in such a spirit of love and compromise that Abram approached the conflict, giving a rational suggestion as to how it might be resolved.

22. The area Lot chose was fertile with sufficient water and pasture land but even more fertile in immorality. Abram's land was not as fertile, but it did allow him to move his vast flocks around without infringing on others' territory. Abram clearly came out ahead.

23. Genesis 12:1 calls for Abram to leave his people and the household of which Lot had been a part. 1 Corinthians 11:19 suggests that a less-than-righteous attitude like Lot's will eventually surface.

24. God promises Abram all the land he can see in every direction (v. 14). This would belong to his descendants forever (v. 15). Furthermore, the Lord would multiply Abram's line to the point no one could count them (v. 16). Accordingly, the two main promises involved land and offspring.

25. Many participants will find, upon reflection, that God has rewarded them with peace of mind and perhaps in even more material ways as they live in harmony with His will.

26. Participants may share comments. Stress especially the enormous grace of the Lord in His dealings with Abram. Despite Abram's sins and unworthiness, the Lord poured out His blessings on his servant. We can personalize this when we recall that God's mercy on Abram was also mercy on us—our Savior came from Abram's line, the line that the Lord preserved in mercy for us!

The Lifeline Is Focused

Genesis 14–16

Preparing for the Session

Central Focus

This sixth lesson is a study in power and weakness, victory and defeat, as God reaffirms His promises to Abram, who continues to exhibit a great faith punctuated by occasional bouts of human doubt.

Objectives

That the participant, as a child of God and with the Holy Spirit's help, will be led to

1. acknowledge God's hand in the victories of His people;

2. recognize the need to avoid human alliances that might lead God's people away from Him;

3. learn how to trust God for the impossible, instead of foolishly taking things into our own hands.

Small-Group Discussion Helps

Review question: The tower builders arrogantly sought to make a name for themselves and refused to disperse across the earth as God had commanded. The tower may also have been used for divination and idolatry. Abram showed faith in God when he left the security of family behind and went to the place where God directed him.

Day 1 • Genesis 14:1–16

1. The invaders were (a) Amraphel of Shinar, (b) Arioch of Ellasar, (c) Kedorlaomer of Elam, and (d) Tidal of Goiim. The opposing kings were (e) Bera of Sodom, (f) Birsha of Gomorrah, (g) Shinab of Admah, (h) Shemeber of Zeboiim, and (i) the ruler of Bela (also known as Zoar). Archaeological discoveries and linguistic studies

of such names, as well as the military destruction of that period, attest once again to the accuracy of the Bible.

2. The time to pay the piper always comes. Lot should have known better than to choose to live among the wicked Sodomites, despite the apparent economic advantages of the location.

3. (a) James encourages us to pray for God's wisdom and discernment. (b) The psalmist points us to the study of God's Word for light and knowledge. (c) Solomon urges us to be receptive to the advice of wise friends.

4. (a) As he considered Lot's selfish and foolish choice of where to live, Abram could have said, "Lot made his bed; now let him lie in it." Abram lived far outside these cities; therefore, it was not really his concern. He also could have compared his few fighting men to the invading army and decided that he would have no chance of rescuing Lot. (b) However, when we know what is right and do not do it, there is no excuse. Let volunteers comment.

5. The number of men Abram could muster from his own household indicates great wealth and influence. However, even Abram's power was meager compared to this invasion force of enemy soldiers. Jehoshaphat prayed to God, who is stronger than even the strongest enemy. Abram's eyes were on God, who fought for Abram and won, just as God gave Gideon and his band of 300 men the victory over a vastly superior force.

6. On our own, we are pitifully outgunned by the supernatural forces of darkness, but when we don the full armor of God, we can defeat even Satan and his demonic hordes.

Day 2 • Genesis 14:17–24

7. Melchizedek brought bread and wine to meet the physical needs of Abram and his men, while also bringing a special blessing from the Lord to meet their spiritual needs. How good God is to His weary, battle-worn children!

8. As our High Priest, Jesus is the one who intercedes for us and gives us the right to approach God's throne. He has brought His sacrificial love and forgiveness. That is why we confidently expect His mercy and grace in time of need.

9. **Challenge question.** Psalm 110:4 looked to a future day in which the Levitical priesthood of Aaron would be replaced by a better and very different one—one in which the priest would also be a king. Melchizedek is a type; Christ is the fulfillment. The major comparison in Hebrews shows us that just as Melchizedek exercised his priesthood, not because he belonged to a priestly family but because he was appointed by God directly, so also Jesus gained His priesthood, not through the line of Levi but by God's direct appointment. Jesus is our King of righteousness, the King of peace, our King forever!

10. The lesser always gives the tithe to the greater. Abram's tithe shows, then, that the priestly order of Melchizedek was greater than the Levitical priesthood (which came from Abraham). We have something for which to thank God every day of our lives and not only on special occasions.

11. The king of Salem came out with his arms full and ready to give, but the king of Sodom came out with his arms empty and ready to take.

12. "Possession is nine-tenths of the law." "To the victor belong the spoils." According to the customs of his day, Abram could have kept everything, but he was not only generous, he was cautious. "Not even a thread" would he take from the Sodomites, because there would always be strings attached to such transactions. Perhaps 1 Corinthians 10:23–24 might apply to the use and distribution of Abram's booty, as well as our bounty.

Day 3 • Genesis 15:1–6

13. Evidently, this is the fifth time God revealed Himself to Abram. You might refer the group to Psalm 3:3, which pictures God shielding or protecting us from our enemies as a king protects his people. In Psalm 5:12 we see God surrounding His people with a gigantic shield of grace.

14. Abram addresses God as Sovereign Lord or, more literally, Lord Yahweh. He is Lord because He is Abram's master, and He is Yahweh (God's personal name in Hebrew) because of the covenant promises God gave to Abram. The adoption of a slave to inherit the property assured a childless couple that they would be taken care of in their old age and would receive a proper burial. God's promise becomes more specific as He assures Abram (a) he would have a natural heir, not an adopted one, and (b) eventually, his offspring would be as numerous as the stars.

15. The Gentiles who believe are also considered to be Abraham's offspring and, therefore, are numbered among those stars.

16. God's assurance that He will always be with us removes any reason to fear. He is present to hear our prayers and to help us.

Day 4 • Genesis 15:7–21

17. Abram's request is in reference to possession of the land and is not connected to the promise of a natural heir. Nevertheless, his request—like Hezekiah's request—should not be viewed as doubt or a lack of faith. The request simply expressed a heartfelt longing to see God fulfill His promises by confirming His covenant in a visible way. In fact, to refuse a proffered sign can demonstrate a lack of faith, as in the case of King Ahaz in Isaiah 7:10–14! After all, God Himself has set the precedent for such confirmations of covenants by the rainbow in Genesis 9:12–13. Today, our Lord in grace gives us the Sacrament of the Altar as a visible sign confirming His presence among us. In Christ's body and blood we receive the forgiveness of sins, just as the new covenant promises.

18. (a) Only God walked through the butchered animal halves because God's promises to Abram were unconditional. The Lord would make good on all His promises. Abram only received God's good gifts—doing nothing to deserve or earn them. (b) The good news was that Abram would live to a ripe old age and die in peace. Furthermore, his descendants would inherit the Promised Land and enter it with great possessions. The bad news was that those descendants first would be enslaved for four generations and would have to fight the Amorites for the land.

19. (a) The smoking firepot was used for baking. It was a large earthenware jar into which charcoal was placed. Dough was stuck to the outside and baked in this way. Smoke and fire are symbolic of God's presence. (b) The children of Israel witnessed that in their wilderness wanderings when they were accompanied by the pillar of fire and when God manifested Himself on Sinai by the cloud of smoke.

20. During Solomon's reign Israel's boundaries approached the limits stated in Genesis 15:18–21.

21. **Challenge question.** (a) The parallels between our time and Old Testament days are great in terms of immorality, but we also must be careful in such comparisons, because God no longer deals with a specific national group or a particular geographical plot of land. Today God's people are contained not within a political realm (the nation of Israel) but a spiritual realm (the church). Nevertheless, God's judgment surely will descend upon wicked rulers and nations. (b) God may visit nations already in this age through natural disasters, war, and other means. Certainly all the wicked who do not repent and turn in faith to Christ in this age will experience everlasting punishment in hell. God also may chasten believers who sin, but always with the intention of leading us to repentance. Even then, He first comes to us in His Word to confront our sin and our need for repentance. Tragic circumstances may happen to us if we refuse to listen and obey. However, make sure participants understand that God never punishes us for our sins—Jesus took all our punishment in our place. We need not fear that He will kill our children or ruin our finances. When evil things happen to us, we can run *to* Him for help. We need not run *from* Him in fear!

22. Although God has the right to destroy swiftly such immorality and evil, in patience He allots additional time for repentance on the part of sinners. Ask the members of the group to consider how patient God has been with them!

. . . .

Day 5 • Genesis 16

23. Be sure to emphasize the decade of apprehension that Abram and Sarai endured. From a human stand-

point we can understand this plan. But while God promised to bless Ishmael, He did not accept him as the bearer of the promised Seed. Instead, God firmly repeats His promise that Abram will have a son by his wife, Sarai.

24. It is important that every stone be in place. Every member of God's church is important and vital to the structure. Accept other comparisons based on the text.

25. The members of your LifeLight group will come up with many reasons each of these individuals should be held responsible for the unfortunate consequences of acting outside God's will. For example: (a) Sarai's immoral initiative, (b) Hagar's haughty character, and (c) Abram's abdication of spiritual leadership in his household.

26. Hagar is to return to her mistress and submit to her (just as St. Paul counseled Onesimus to go back to Philemon). God promises her countless descendants and, in particular, a son who would be named Ishmael, one of the forefathers of the Arab nations, which would be in conflict with the Jews.

27. Like Isaac, we are the children of promise by the free woman (Sarah) because we are freed from the Law by the power of God's Spirit.

The Lifeline in Abraham

Genesis 17–19

Preparing for the Session

Central Focus

These three chapters reiterate a continuing theme in Genesis: judgment and grace. Judgment is demonstrated in the destruction of wicked Sodom and Gomorrah, but grace is in God's gift of the covenant sign of circumcision and in His deliverance of Lot and his daughters from destruction.

Objectives

That the participant, as a child of God and with the Holy Spirit's help, will be led to

1. treasure Baptism as God's covenant of grace;

2. better understand the power and process of intercessory prayer and grow in commitment to such prayer;

3. understand and rely on God's grace in the midst of His judgment.

Small-Group Discussion Helps

Review question: Like Christ, Melchizedek was a priest, but not a Levite. Like Christ, Melchizedek was king as well as priest. Like Christ, Melchizedek was king of Salem ("peace").

Day 1 • Genesis 17

1. God expects us to be blameless, perfect, but that can only be attained when Christ transfers His perfection to our record. Abram's prior reactions to the covenant had been premature and immature; he attempted to father an heir in a way other than according to God's plan. In Genesis 17:1 the Lord reminded Abram of the seriousness of the covenant and urged Abram to treat it with utmost seriousness. The salvation of the world hung in the balance. Had Abram disqualified himself through recklessness and unbelief (as he nearly did in Genesis 16), the Lord still would have found a way to bring salvation. But Abram and Sarai may have lost their honored place as carriers of that covenant. In Genesis 17:1 the Lord impresses this truth upon Abram's heart.

2. Let volunteers comment. Perhaps some in your group have endured times when the Lord seemed silent. During such times the Holy Spirit wants to strengthen us as He strengthened Abram—through His Word, the comfort and promises He so freely has given to us as He gave these to Abram.

3. Abram ("exalted father") becomes Abraham ("father of a multitude"). His new name emphasizes the covenant promise of descendants as numerous as the stars. Because Sarai would become the mother of kings and nations, her name appropriately became Sarah ("princess"). Although circumcision was not unique to the Hebrews, it was now to be set apart as the spiritual sign of those who were obedient to God's covenant. Later, it would also become a national sign (Exodus 4:24–26; Joshua 5:2–8) that was sometimes abused or misunderstood as a replacement for the faith God counts as righteousness.

4. **Challenge question.** Circumcision was a *sign* of the covenant; Baptism *is* the covenant by which forgiveness of sins and the Holy Spirit are bestowed. Furthermore, Baptism is for all believers—males and females.

5. Abraham's laughter may have been from joy, but it still sounded rather skeptical, didn't it? Even after these specific words from the Lord, Abraham still clings to his plan that Ishmael would be his heir.

6. When we skeptically take matters into our own hands, it is upsetting to discover that we have been on the wrong track. We may even become hostile when God tries to put us back on the right track and reshapes our plans so they mesh with His eternal will.

7. (a) God is very clear in stating that Sarah would be the mother of the promised heir! God assures Abraham

that Sarah's son would, in turn, have descendants who also would be part of this covenant. Ishmael would also be blessed with many offspring. Furthermore, Abraham's heir, whom he was to name Isaac, would be born within the year. Note that Abraham follows God's instructions on that very day. (b) Let volunteers comment. As you discuss the issue be sure to stress that power for the kind of instant obedience Abraham demonstrated comes only from the Gospel. It might be easy to view Abraham through rose-colored glasses, thinking somehow he made himself a giant of faith. But note the context of these very verses! We see in 17:2–22 the unconditional Good News God lavished on an undeserving Abraham. That Good News empowered the obedience of verses 23–27.

Day 2 • Genesis 18:1–15

8. Consider how Abraham's words indicate honor, as to men of greater rank. Also, he butchered and prepared a calf and provided a large amount of bread, plus butter and milk.

9. Times change, and the way hospitality is demonstrated in one culture may be different than in another. However, the basic attitude and obligation of hospitality remains, for by welcoming someone in Christ's name we welcome Christ. What an honor!

10. The text indicates this was the Lord, accompanied by two angels.

11. Sarah was to play a vital role in fulfilling this aspect of the covenant, and because she was listening to their words, she needed to be reassured of the specific promise that she would bear this heir within a year.

12. Nothing is too difficult for almighty God. Our pitiful doubt and unbelief cannot derail His gracious promises. How comforting!

Day 3 • Genesis 18:16–33

13. Abraham and his offspring were to set an example of righteousness and justice in the land. What was about to happen to Sodom would be an important object lesson that Abraham would always remember and would teach his descendants.

14. Abraham was God's friend; his was—by the Lord's grace—a very close relationship with the true God.

15. We also are God's friends in Christ Jesus. Therefore, we may come to Him in prayer, including prayers on behalf of others whom we are to love as Christ loved us.

16. Here is a mystery of love too deep for human comprehension. Scripture indicates that God often waits to act in response to our prayers!

17. **Challenge question.** We have an obligation to pray for others. However, as it has been said, "too often we pray as if we must overcome God's reluctance rather than seize upon His willingness." In fact, the Lord urges us to pray for ourselves and for others. Since God's will is always for our life and blessing, since He desires all to be saved and to come to know His truth, why would we want to pray for a change in His good and gracious will? Rather, we pray that His loving will might be accomplished in and through us and in and through those for whom we pray.

Day 4 • Genesis 19:1–14

18. Authority and power are given, but respect must be earned. Lot does not appear to have had much influence on the Sodomites.

19. Lot's future sons-in-law refused to take him seriously, and his wife was so attached to the luxuries of Sodom that she also ignored his warning. There seems to be little evidence that Lot served as the spiritual leader in his household.

20. Purposely placing ourselves and our families into places of temptation makes it difficult to be *in* the world, yet *not of* the world.

21. Homosexuality is totally incompatible with God's Word, no matter how some people attempt to rationalize or even Christianize such an abomination.

22. The blood of Jesus Christ cleanses us of any sin. Even homosexuality can be defeated by the power of Jesus Christ in a person's life.

23. That Lot would be willing to deliver his daughters to the lust of the men of Sodom (perhaps considering this the lesser of two evils) shows an almost unthinkable willingness to compromise with evil.

Day 5 • Genesis 19:15–38

24. A strong case could be made that Lot's hesitancy demonstrated a lack of faith, showing he was no better than the rest; the angels had to drag him out of town! Here again we see the workings of a merciful God in saving Lot despite Lot's sinfulness.

25. By definition, a disciple is a follower, not a quitter. To abandon Christ is to be unworthy of Him. This, of course, is Law, and it chills us to consider our own fickleness. When we see our weakness, we flee to God's infinite grace, relying on His pardon and on His power to live an influential life of commitment and love for Christ.

26. Thoughts may range from satisfaction that justice was done, to sadness, and to awe of God's power.

27. Lot's life was spared because of God's covenant with Abraham and because of Lot's relationship with Abraham.

28. Evidently Lot was still numbered among the righteous, despite his lapses. This can provide great comfort to us as we realize our own guilt before God.

29. The Ammonites and Moabites, descended from Lot's union with his two daughters, became bitter enemies of God's chosen people.

30. Answers will vary.

The Lifeline through Isaac

Genesis 20–22

Preparing for the Session

Central Focus

Considering Abraham's dealings with Abimelech and Hagar, "history repeats itself" might be an appropriate theme for this study. However, Abraham's testing, central to the covenant lifeline theme of Genesis, dominates this lesson.

Objectives

That the participant, as a child of God and with the Holy Spirit's help, will be led to

1. learn from mistakes rather than repeat them;

2. recognize God's grace and provision, active even toward those whom others have rejected;

3. trust God more completely in times of testing;

4. thank God for the sacrifice of His Son.

For the Small-Group Leader

You might mention in the course of your group's discussion that past sins seemed to resurface in the life of Abraham and Sarah, just as they do in our lives today.

During the discussion session remain aware of the passing time. Pace the discussion of the study questions to keep the study flowing and to allow enough time for covering the entire unit.

Small-Group Discussion Helps

Review question: The Lord assured Abraham and Sarah they would have a son within a year. God also told Abraham that He was about to investigate and deal with Sodom and Gomorrah.

Day 1 • Genesis 20:1–18

1. In each incident Abraham used the ruse of Sarah's half-sister relationship to protect himself from the deadly threat of a pagan king, and Sarah went along with it. Furthermore, each time Abraham ended up materially richer. We are not told how the Pharaoh discovered the secret. Abimelech was not allowed to touch Sarah and was warned directly by God in a dream.

2. If Abimelech had had sexual relations with Sarah, the promise in Genesis 18:10 would have been suspect. Therefore, the lifeline to the Messiah was endangered by this action.

3. Abimelech and his household were once again able to have children.

4. A Christian's lifestyle is a testimony itself and must be holy so the integrity of our actions will substantiate the integrity of our words.

5. (a) Abraham claims this is a place of no true religion, and he points out that Sarah is his half-sister. (b) In Ephesians 4, Paul says that believers are to speak the truth in love. Proverbs 17 tells us that lies never speak well of any person. In fact it is better not to say anything at all than to lie.

Day 2 • Genesis 21:1–7

6. Both Paul and the author of Hebrews attest to the faith of these ancient believers. Nevertheless, Moses clearly reveals the faults and faithless acts of Abraham and Sarah. If God used sinners such as Abraham and Sarah to accomplish His will, we know He can accomplish His work through us.

7. The spiritual fruit of patience belongs to every believer (Galatians 5:22), but it is exercised in varying degrees from day to day. Considering the number of years that elapsed between God's promise and the fulfillment of that promise, Abraham and Sarah were probably more patient than most of us would be.

8. If God says He will do something, we can be sure that it is as good as done; it will be done at the very time and in the very way God has promised.

9. As with Ishmael, God had selected the name Abraham gave his son—undoubtedly in view of the laughter of both Sarah and Abraham when God promised them a son. Isaac literally means "he laughs."

10. A strong case can be made for either choice.

11. Without circumcision Isaac would not have been part of the covenant line that would lead to the Messiah.

Day 3 • Genesis 21:8–21

12. Evidently, Ishmael learned how to ridicule others. The 14-year-old must have still considered himself Abraham's heir or must have been jealous of the new heir.

13. Sarah's anger once again resulted in cruelty. Nevertheless, Galatians 4:30 views Sarah's suggestion as inspired.

14. Jesus tells us to pray for those who ridicule or even persecute us. Ask your group for what they would pray: understanding? revenge? a change of attitude? something else?

15. Abraham had a deep love and affection for Ishmael, his son.

16. God demonstrated a deep love for Ishmael by promising to make a great nation out of his offspring. He, too, would produce 12 tribes or nations.

17. God not only answered the cries of Ishmael in the wilderness by giving him water, but He also was with him as he grew up in the desert.

18. **Challenge question.** In this section of Galatians Paul contrasts grace and Law, faith and works. He uses Hagar and Sarah, as well as Ishmael and Isaac, allegorically. Hagar and Ishmael represent the yoke of the Law, while Sarah and Isaac represent the freedom of the Gospel. As those who live by faith instead of works, we are like Isaac, children of grace, living under Gospel freedom. However, those who live by works will be cast out, just as Hagar and Ishmael were cast out.

19. (a) Isaac came to Abraham through faith in God's promises. We also are children of God's promise, like Isaac, (b) through faith in Christ Jesus.

Day 4 • Genesis 21:22–34

20. (a) Hagar obtained a wife for Ishmael from Egypt, (b) a predictable choice since she was an Egyptian. (c) However, Ishmael's wife would not have believed in God and might well have led her husband away from Him.

21. (a) Abraham sealed the covenant he made with Abimelech by giving him sheep and cattle. (b) Seven ewe lambs were to be a living reminder to Abimelech of how Abraham had dug the well and of how Abimelech had agreed that the well belonged to Abraham.

22. (a) Abraham planted a tamarisk tree as a visible expression of his gratitude to God. There he called on God in prayer and worshiped Him. (b) We may express our thankfulness to God by our worship, offerings, and the service we give to others.

Day 5 • Genesis 22

23. God tells us in these passages that He tempts no one. However, He does test His people. Temptation is intended to destroy a person's faith. Testing is intended to strengthen it. If the test becomes too severe—so much so that it would lead to temptation—God promises a way of escape. Abraham's trial demonstrated a strong faith.

24. **Challenge question.** As son given up by the father, Isaac helps us understand John 3:16 and Romans 8:32. Sacrificed in Isaac's place, the ram represents Christ.

25. Abraham believed in the physical resurrection of the dead, just as our faith is founded in the physical resurrection of Christ, who will raise us from the dead on the Last Day.

26. (a) Both passages refer to the sacrifice of a living human being—Genesis 22 the sacrifice of Isaac, Romans 12:1–2 the sacrifice of our own bodies. (b) God desires a living sacrifice from us also—the sacrifice of our lives to Him in everything we do or say.

27. Rebekah would become Isaac's wife and the servant of God's promise to give countless descendants to Abraham.

28. Abraham lived in faith, sometimes displaying that faith remarkably. At other times he failed. Through it all God demonstrated His faithfulness by sustaining, guiding, and blessing Abraham and by keeping His promise to bless all nations through Abraham's seed.

The Lifeline Expands

Genesis 23:1–25:11

Preparing for the Session

Central Focus

This final lesson in our study of the first half of Genesis encompasses the death of Sarah and Abraham but also the marriage of Isaac and Rebekah. The promise to Abraham will go on through his descendants.

Objectives

That the participant, as a child of God and with the Holy Spirit's help, will be led to

1. see this earth only as a temporary home for those who hold citizenship in heaven through their Baptism;

2. look to the guidance of God in the selection of a Christian mate;

3. praise God that His covenant promises do not die, even when people do.

For the Small-Group Leader

Several questions in the study leaflet give the small-group leader an opportunity to assess the bonding that has taken place during the past nine weeks. Be sensitive to feelings members of the group may have about old age and marriage. Participants should be encouraged to continue with the next nine-week LifeLight course, which studies the last half of Genesis.

Small-Group Discussion Helps

Review question: God gave Abraham an opportunity to show that he loved God more than anything or anyone, even more than his dear son Isaac, who represented all of Abraham's hopes. Abraham also showed that he believed God could raise the dead. Note that the "test" was for Abraham's sake, not the Lord's. Omniscient, God already knew what Abraham would do.

Day 1 • Genesis 23

1. Peter holds up not only Abraham but also Sarah as examples of great faith. Answers from the group may point to Sarah's faithfulness and willing submission to Abraham during their 60-plus years of marriage or Peter's emphasis on the inner beauty of Sarah, which encompasses a "gentle and quiet spirit," or the hope she placed in God's covenant of a promised child who would lead to the promised Messiah.

2. An alien was a nomadic foreigner with no property or place to call home. A stranger was a squatter with a home but no land property. Consider Leviticus 25:23 as God's reminder that no matter how long we stay on this earth, we are simply passing through, because heaven is our home.

3. What can each of us do to help one another experience the actual family relationship into which our Savior has placed us in His church? Time for some brainstorming! But do not let it end there. Put your ideas into action. "I was a stranger and you invited Me in" (Matthew 26:35).

4. If a member of your LifeLight group still feels like a stranger after nine sessions, something is wrong, even if that person may not be willing to verbalize the estrangement. Use your love and creativity to remedy the situation. Those who do view themselves as part of the group will share terms such as *comfortable, caring, friends, prayer partner,* and so forth.

5. Sarah, Abraham, Isaac, Rebekah, Leah, and Jacob were buried in this family tomb. If someone asks about Rachel, see Genesis 35:19–20.

6. Abraham never lost sight of the true promised land, heaven.

7. We also can be assured that, from the day of our Baptism, God made us citizens of heaven and heirs of eternal life.

Day 2 • Genesis 24:1–9

8. (a) It was vital that a wife for Isaac believe in the same true God and take part in the way of life compatible with Isaac's. Abraham himself was not permitted to return to Mesopotamia to find such a mate. (b) Marrying a pagan Canaanite could lead Isaac away from the true God, just as many a pagan mate has done with a believing spouse. So the search for Isaac's wife began in Abraham's own family.

9. (a) Whatever else this list may include, a top priority should be faith in Christ alone for eternal life. (b) A question for personal reflection. (c) A Christian can pray for an unbelieving partner and provide a positive witness in word and deed.

10. The promise of the accompanying presence of the angel of the Lord—in other words, God Himself—made Abraham confident that the right mate would be found.

11. When we depend on human wisdom instead of divine guidance we most often get into trouble. Those who trust in God to lead them will find the perfect answer at the end of each path.

Day 3 • Genesis 24:10–27

12. The supplies required for such a long journey would have been carried by many camels. Also, the servant took valuables to be used as gifts. Finally, the men who rode along to protect these valuables from bandits required mounts.

13. The servant's prayers and worship directed to the God of Abraham demonstrate that this servant—as in most ancient households—worshiped the same God as did his master. Obviously, this servant did so eagerly and voluntarily.

14. **Challenge question.** (a) We Christians frequently ask God to guide us when we are working through a difficult decision. The choice of a spouse is obviously such a decision—but so also are the choice of a career or job, the decision to have a certain type of medical treatment, and countless other decisions, large and small. Members of your group will no doubt think of many such decisions that lead us to pray for God's guidance. (b) Like the

servant we may see God's guidance in outward circumstances (vv. 18–19), in His revealed will (v. 27), and in the experience of inward peace and assurance (v. 26).

15. How often God meets our needs before we either recognize the need or get around to asking Him to meet that need! Awareness of this will surely encourage us to pray to God more readily.

16. Rebekah was Abraham's grandniece and Isaac's cousin.

17. Rebekah was a virgin, a relative, hospitable, and hardworking; she demonstrated initiative, was beautiful, and had other attractive qualities. Obviously, this was a match made in heaven!

Day 4 • Genesis 24:28–67

18. Laban's comments in verses 31 and 50 indicate that Laban and his family knew and worshiped the true God.

19. (a) God intends that one's primary loyalty be given to one's spouse. (b) This is true also for married couples today.

20. Rebekah's marriage to Abraham's son made her part of the process by which God would fulfill His promise to give Abraham descendants as numerous as the stars.

21. Isaac may have been praying that the mission of the servant would be a success and that he would bring back a godly mate for him.

22. (a) This is a good opportunity to talk about the importance of personal devotions and group Bible study. The individual, daily study in LifeLight provides the opportunity for talking to God and listening to His Word. Remind the students of this blessing that is theirs as they prayerfully meditate on the daily LifeLight texts. (b) Unless we purposely set aside regular time, our devotional life becomes sporadic, at best. Designating a particular quiet place where there is less chance of disruption also enhances our devotional time.

23. Rebekah brought love and comfort to Isaac after the loss of his mother.

Day 5 • Genesis 25:1–11

24. Abraham was to become the father of the Hebrew nation and also of many other nations. Genesis 25:1–4 lists some of those nations, including Arab nations. In keeping with the culture of Abraham's world, Keturah was a "lesser wife" or "concubine." The Lord designed marriage as a lifelong union between one man and one woman. However, He allowed multiple wives throughout part of Old Testament history. This practice almost always resulted in family troubles and a good deal of misery for the parties involved. We will encounter the practice of polygamy again in Genesis, Part 2 of the LifeLight series. If anyone questions the practice, share the information above. If you need a fuller explanation, ask your pastor. Note that the lecture for this session also addresses the issue.

25. **Challenge question.** As legal firstborn, Isaac was entitled to a double portion of the inheritance. The other sons were given their shares and sent away so there would be no future claims on the inheritance or undue influence by some of whom would turn out to be Israel's enemies, such as the Midianites.

26. A long life gives a believer a longer opportunity to share the Gospel as well as the godly wisdom that comes with years of Scripture study.

27. Funerals create enough emotional stress without the additional trauma of embittered relatives trying to make amends. Besides, any resolution does no good for the deceased, who no longer is around to enjoy it. On the other hand, family members may find themselves together, face-to-face at a funeral. The Holy Spirit might use the pain of grief to help mourners open up to one another in confession and forgiveness. Our Lord always desires the reconciliation of His people with one another. Accordingly, we will want to use any opportunity to make peace that He provides.

28. *Now* is always the time to resolve differences.

29. This question is the final opportunity for members of the LifeLight group to look back over their in-depth studies in this first half of Genesis and to grab hold of a golden nugget of wisdom they can take with them into Genesis, Part 2.